Rollie Burns

ROLLIE BURNS

OR

AN ACCOUNT *of the* RANCHING INDUSTRY
ON THE SOUTH PLAINS

By

W. C. HOLDEN

TEXAS A&M UNIVERSITY PRESS
COLLEGE STATION

Library of Congress Cataloging-in-Publication Data
Holden, William Curry, 1896–
    Rollie Burns, or, An account of the ranching industry on
the south Plains.
    (A Southwest landmark; no. 4)
    Originally published: Dallas, Tex.: Southwest Press, 1932.
    Includes index.
    1. Burns, Rollie, 1857–1945. 2. Ranchers—Texas—
Biography. 3. Ranch life—Texas—History. 4. Texas—
Biography. 5. Texas—Social life and customs. I. Title.
II. Title: Rollie Burns. III. Title: Account of the ranching
industry on the south Plains. IV. Series.
F391.B93H65   1986   976.4'06'0924   85-20799
ISBN 0-89096-261-8 (c); ISBN 1-58544-055-8 (p)

Manufactured in the United States of America

To

MARY EMMA BOLES BURNS

INTRODUCTION TO THE

1986 EDITION

WILLIAM Curry Holden and J. Evetts Haley are names that are synonymous with the finest in West Texas history. Both participated in the founding of the two major historical journals that serve the region. Both figured prominently in the establishment of three historical research collections that preserve the area's rich heritage. Collectively they have written to date seventeen major books and hundreds of articles and pamphlets on southwestern history.

Their admirers know that Holden and Haley worked together to produce one study, *The Flamboyant Judge*, but most readers do not know that they also worked separately nearly fifty years earlier to bring about *Rollie Burns*, a tremendous contribution to West Texas history and literature. While Holden gives opening-line credit to Haley in his introduction to *Rollie Burns*, only Burns and Haley knew the full role played by the latter in the book's creation.

Rollie Burns had turned sixty-eight years old in 1925, and like so many old-timers, he decided that it was time he started writing down his reminiscences. As a prominent citizen of Lubbock and one of the South Plains' earliest residents (he arrived in 1881), Burns had no trouble convincing the local newspaper editor to publish some of his stories. These accounts caught the eye of young Evetts Haley, the new field secretary for the fledgling Panhandle-Plains Historical Society in Canyon. Haley collected some of Burns's ranch records, interviewed the old cowboy in 1926 and 1927, and soon became Burns's good friend. Burns sent Haley stories about his experiences in West Texas and with Haley's encouragement began to compile his reminiscences in narrative form.

In the spring of 1929, Haley sent Burns a complimentary copy of his new study on the historic XIT Ranch. A month later, impressed by Haley's work, Burns returned the favor by sending Haley the first "installment" of his own efforts. Haley quickly responded by marking corrections, making some suggestions for improvements, and having the manuscript typed. Within a month, Burns sent Haley three more chapters.

Haley's recommendations were courteous but pointed: "During the first two or three installments your narrative flowed with remarkable sequence, but now it is jumping around from incident to incident. Let the narrative be as coherent as possible." Two months later, following additional submissions from Burns, Haley noted, "Some of your stories are still out of joint." Burns was not discouraged. "If this needs doctoring, you are the doctor and will cure it," he wrote Haley, and asked him to write the introduction when the work was completed.

Like many aspiring authors, Burns envisioned some profit from his work. But Haley was quick to warn that Burns would have difficulty in finding a publisher who would allow a royalty and suggested that Burns try to make a deal with the *Lubbock Avalanche* to print his articles, save the type, and then print them all as a book.

While Burns continued to write stories, Haley moved in January, 1930, from Canyon to Austin to work as a field researcher for the University of Texas. He soon learned that the Panhandle-Plains Historical Society faced new competition for West Texas materials. In the fall of 1929, the Texas Technological College Library acquired its first manuscript collection, the records of the Spur Ranch. Then, in April, 1930, through the work of Holden, it acquired the Matador Ranch records. Meanwhile, following a quick April trip from Austin to the Panhandle, Haley stopped in Lubbock to visit Burns and there learned that "some of the Tech people" had been after Burns to get his ranch papers back from Canyon. Haley bluntly confronted Holden with what he had learned when the two met in Dallas at the annual meeting of the Texas State Historical Association. Haley later reported the conversation to L. F. Sheffy, his successor at Canyon: "I wanted them to know that if such was to be their policies, I would guarantee to be damned sure to give them everything they wanted in return. . . . I think there is plenty of room for all of us there to work in the history of that section, and I would like to be there for several reasons, prominent among which would be to help keep Tech from getting ahead of us. . . . Of course all of this shows that West Texas has suddenly become a very popular historical field, and that we have a lot of competition on our hands."

Before Haley could resume work on Burns's manu-
script, problems arose in Lubbock over *The XIT*, and
Haley soon found himself in court defending his book.
The matter required much of 1931 to settle, but by
September he was ready to resume work on Burns's
manuscript. He wrote Burns that he hoped he could
get it published in the next issue of the *Panhandle-
Plains Historical Review*.

As the Depression worsened, Burns looked to the
publication of his manuscript to provide some income,
but he learned from Haley that cost of reprints of the
Review would have to come from his own pocket. Therefore, he decided to pursue another course.

Burns sent his manuscript to J. Frank Dobie, who
quickly responded to say that Burns's best hope was
already in Lubbock in the person of William Curry
Holden. In the fall of 1931, Holden was thirty-five
years old and beginning his third year of teaching at
Texas Tech. The year before, his dissertation was published as *Alkali Trails* by Southwest Press of Dallas.
Burns decided that Holden was the right man to help
him. Holden remembered well his first visit with the
old cowboy: "One day at noon, somebody knocked on
the front door. There stood this blocky little man with
a mustache, a rather dignified little person. . . . He had
with him a manuscript."

Holden told Burns that he would take a look at his
story. "It may have been a little crude," Holden recalled, "but it was the real McCoy." He promptly wrote
Haley: "I do not want to interfere with anything that

someone else has already started; therefore, before I do anything on his manuscript, I would like to know if you have any intentions of any kind concerning it." Apparently, Haley responded to Holden that he had no reservations about Holden taking the task, but he was abrupt with Burns: "I was rather surprised that you had decided to let Holden work on your manuscript. I am sure that he has more time than I have just now, but was anxious to do anything I could to help you."

Burns interpreted Haley's tone as anger. "Friend Evetts," he responded, "I would rather burn the manuscript than to lose your friendship." Haley hastened to ease the old man's fears: "Please feel that I have no ill-feeling in regard to the manuscript. As I wrote Holden, what I am most interested in is seeing your good interests served. If I can do anything to help the two of you, I will be most happy to do so."

Meanwhile, Holden put Burns to work. "He would come every day at one o'clock, and I'd give him an assignment for the next day—like a seventh grader writing a theme. He knew all the details; he just never thought those things were important." In such a manner, Burns wrote several essays that Holden wove into the old cowboy's original manuscript; then Holden reorganized the topics and, as he later recalled, "wrote [the book] from scratch." Holden started the project in late November, 1931, and eight weeks later had it ready for publication. Southwest Press gladly accepted the manuscript and produced the book in an attractive tan and black cover. Unfortunately, the Press soon fell to the Depression, and Burns's and Holden's only reward was to obtain the unbound copies, which they bound in green covers and distributed the best they could.

Burns's original manuscript, his additional essays, and Holden's handwritten draft are all housed in the Southwest Collection at Texas Tech. A quick perusal through the papers reveals several things about *Rollie Burns*: (1) Holden masterfully carved from rough lumber a fine piece of literature; (2) he "enlivened," as he later admitted, Burns's descriptions by drawing from his own similar experiences of growing up in West Texas; and (3) he was not able to include all of Burns's material, and much remains unused in Burns's papers at the Southwest Collection, the Panhandle-Plains Historical Museum, and the Nita Stewart Haley Library.

Because of the book, Rollie Burns became a household name on the South Plains. The old cowboy lived to enjoy his fame until March 2, 1945, when he died just four weeks before his eighty-eighth birthday. Holden and Haley, of course, are still very much with us, both in good health at eighty-nine and eighty-four, respectively. They have been good friends for over fifty-five years, and in many respects their friend in common, Rollie Burns, drew them together. *Rollie Burns* remains a timeless tribute to their long dedication to West Texas history.

DAVID J. MURRAH

Texas Tech University, July 20, 1985

PREFACE

THIS book should have been written by J. Evetts Haley. It was he who "discovered" Mr. R. C. Burns some years back and who, together with Miss Elizabeth Howard West, encouraged him to begin writing down his experiences. It was not until the fall of 1931 that I became acquainted with Mr. Burns. I found him to be a splendid source for historical information. He was on the Plains before the Indians were forced onto Reservations; he saw the great buffalo herds a year before the first commercial hide hunters entered the Panhandle; he witnessed the development of the cattle industry on the South Plains through the free range phase and then the inclosed ranching period; he saw the big ranch give way to the onslaught of the nesters; he helped found a city, and stood by while agriculture slowly became supreme on the South Plains—a series of experiences which entitle him to the privilege of being called "a pioneer." Few men are to be found today whose active life spans so many phases of West Texas history.

This work is based largely upon Mr. Burns' reminiscences. It is as authentic as his memory is authentic. No doubt errors have crept in, for one's mind at seventy-five is apt to be fallible, especially in regard to dates of events which happened fifty years ago. At one time Mr. Burns had a large collection of records, but most of these were destroyed when his home burned in 1915. Fortunately, about two hundred and fifty of his letters were in an old trunk in the barn at the time, and these were saved. These letters are now deposited with the West Texas State Teachers' College at Canyon. Through the kindness of Mr. Haley and Professor L. F. Sheffy they were loaned to me for the writing of this book. I found them most useful in corroborating the information given me by Mr. Burns.

I have tried to tell the story in Mr. Burns' own diction. That I have not entirely succeeded, I am sure.

I wish to acknowledge the kindness of Miss Lulu Stine, Mr. Cecil Horne, Mr. J. Evetts Haley, and my wife in reading the manuscript. Mr. Burns has worked with me during every phase of its development.

W. C. HOLDEN.

Lubbock, Texas, January 29, 1932.

CONTENTS

CHAPTER I

WE MOVE TO TEXAS

It was the last week in April, 1861. A tall man wearing the blue uniform of a general in the United States army, followed by a number of other men wearing blue uniforms, reined his big black horse in directly in front of my father's moving outfit. General Lane leaned over in his saddle and looked us over for a moment.

In front of our caravan was a hack drawn by two horses. On the seat were father, mother, and I. Father, stocky, sturdy, and with long black mustache, had not shaved for two weeks. Mother, in her calico and sunbonnet which came far out in front of her face, looked tired. I was four years old, and the baby. That's why I was allowed to ride on the seat and help father drive. The hack was filled to a depth of two feet with clothes, boxes of household odds and ends, and bedding. A mattress was spread out on top of all this, and on the mattress rode Mary, Elizabeth, and Florence, whose ages ranged from seven to fourteen.

Behind the hack was our wagon with its heavy wheels and long bed. Four mules were hooked to it.

Two mules could not have pulled the wagon, for it was filled to a depth of five feet with all of our movable plunder. Perched high upon the seat driving was Mose, our negro man. Beside him—black, fat, and shiny, was Lindy. Behind with kinky, tousled heads peering out under the wagon sheet were three little Moses and Lindys. On one side of the wagon was attached a twenty-gallon water barrel, which father had gotten from a saloon keeper. Underneath were several joints of stove pipe. Mother had persistently refused to leave her cook stove. Although it weighed four hundred pounds, it was securely packed in the wagon, perhaps the most precious article in it. Behind the wagon were some extra horses, and my older brothers, Robert, thirteen, and Tom, eleven, were wrangling them.

"Where are you taking those colored people?" asked General Lane in a tone of one who loved "colored people" and hated whites who owned "colored people."

"To Texas."

Father was not disturbed much. He had been sheriff in Nodaway County, Missouri, for the better part of fourteen years. He had taken his chances across the Great Plains during the California gold rush. He had lived through the lawless months of '49 on the Pacific Coast. He had come back to Nodaway County and had been sheriff again. He had hunted runaway slaves in a country in which three-fourths of the population were abolitionists. In his early life he had grown up in Kentucky along side the Austins and Boones, when such characters were holding their own with Indians without the aid of the United States army. So General Lane and his blue-coats didn't ruffle him much. But it was different with mother. She was dreadfully upset, and squeezed me mighty tight.

The general placed father under arrest, and that made mother upset the more. The children became scared and Mose's eyes bulged out. We stayed there all that day and the next. Several times the general questioned father sharply, but he was so busy holding up other outfits and doing a lot of other things that he didn't have time to decide what to do with us. On the third day he took our negroes away from us and told us to go ahead.

From there on we had to manage the wagon. Father drove it; Tom drove the hack, and Bob wrangled the horses. Tom wanted to wrangle the horses too, and he and Bob were always arguing about which one would drive the hack. Occasionally father would make Bob trade places with Tom. As we passed country stores and little towns, everywhere were small groups of men talking about politics and the war that was about to start. News had just come about the fall of Fort Sumter. Bull Run had not yet been fought, but the Yankee forces were gathering at Washington to make a drive on the Rebels. These farmers, small politicians, and local demagogues had strong notions about things. Opinion was pretty well divided. One group around a courthouse or post-office would spit and sputter, and be-damn "that

nigger-loving Lincoln;" another group would accuse
the Rebel, Jeff Davis, and his slave-driving gang,
of everything bad that had happened since the flood.
The air seemed surcharged with a tenseness that made
people restless and uncertain.

We were on our way from Nodaway County in
Northwest Missouri to Collin County, Texas. Father
and his brother-in-law, John Saunders, had pioneered
in Nodaway County. They had founded the county
seat, Maryville, where I was born April 6, 1857. The
tension caused by the abolition question with all the
accompanying squabbles over sovereignty, states'
rights, and the like, made Maryville an uncomfortable place for a Southern man to live during the late
50's—especially since Nodaway County was pre-
dominantly abolitionist and Republican. In the winter
of 1860-1861 a Yankee who had lived several years
in Collin County, Texas, came to Maryville looking
for a trade. He claimed to have a farm, seven hundred head of cattle, and a considerable herd of horses
in Collin County. Father dickered with him awhile,
and traded him, sight unseen, our place in Maryville
for his layout in Texas. We were now on our way
to Texas to settle on a place which we hoped existed.
Father took a big chance, but it was worth something
to get out of a Yankee community.

A few days after leaving Saline County, Missouri,
where we were held up by General Lane, we got
past the settlements. We came through the Ozarks
and the eastern edge of Indian Territory. Several
times we saw Indians, but they didn't molest us any.

But mother breathed a lot easier after we crossed Colbert's Ferry on Red River.

We found the place father had traded for. It had a frame house on it, and was fairly well fixed up, as frontier places went in those days. The cattle were badly scattered, and we never did know how many there were. Father never did even try to round them up. He didn't think much of cattle raising. He said no one could ever do any good in the cattle business unless he was a thief, and father had some old-fashioned notions about honesty. He later traded his claims to the cattle of the brand he had acquired to a Mr. McWhorter for two spans of mules. Father gathered up all the horses he could find. There were not nearly as many as there were supposed to be, but enough for a good start. So father settled down to farming and raising horses.

The Civil War meant hard times to us, though we fared as well as any other frontier families. When the Federal forces were withdrawn from the frontier forts in Texas in the summer of 1861, the Indians went on the rampage, but did not raid as far east as Collin County. They quieted down in 1862 and 1863 when the Frontier Regiment, first commanded by Colonel Norris and later by Colonel Mc-Cord, was stationed in a chain of twenty-odd posts reaching from Red River to the Rio Grande. In 1864 frontier defense was reorganized. A home guard system was established. The frontier was divided into three districts, and the men of military age in the exposed counties were exempted from

service in the Confederate army and were formed
into local militia units. Colonel Throckmorton of
Gainesville was the commander of our district. For
almost a year after the Confederates surrendered in
the spring of 1865, there was no frontier defense at
all, until the posts were reoccupied by Federal troops
under General Phil Sheridan. During this time people suffered dreadfully. The Indians went wild; they
raided, burned and stole. Before the war some settlements had extended a hundred miles west of Collin
County, but by January, 1866, the settlers had fallen
back, and Collin County was again on the frontier.

My grandfather and all my father's brothers were
in the Confederate army. Grandfather was a captain.
My father's youngest brother was killed in one of
the last battles. When the war was over, my grandfather came to Texas and left with us a negro boy
whom he had with him as a servant throughout the
war. Hambone was a little older than I, and we
played, rode, worked, fished, and fought together
for several years.

In 1867, after we had been in Collin County six
years, father decided to move back to Missouri. He
thought times were more prosperous up there. The
new Reconstruction measures were making things appear mighty gloomy in Texas, and he just wanted to
go back. We packed up and started. This time we had
two wagons. The stork had been busy since we got to
Texas. Now we had Jerry, Maggie, and Maud. I
could hardly wait to get started. I was ten years old,
and had learned to ride pretty well for a kid of

that age. We had a hundred and fifty head of horses to drive, and that job fell to Tom, Hambone and myself.

The most thrilling event on this trip was a stampede. After we had been on the road through Indian Territory about ten days, we met an outfit coming south with a bunch of horses. When the two herds got close together, they stampeded, ran together, and headed for the West. Tom, Hambone, and I took after them with all the speed we could muster. The herd almost lost us, but we managed to stay in sight. By taking short cuts we finally managed to catch up. The horses had gotten over their scare; and when we came up, they divided into their respective herds and one herd turned one direction, and the other another. Cattle won't do that. When two herds mix, they have to be cut again. Mother certainly did look relieved when we got back with our herd. She had been on pins ever since we had gone over the hill and disappeared.

A few days after this we met an old neighbor of ours coming south from Nodaway County. He and father had a long talk. When they got through father came around and said, "Well, we're heading back for Texas." He faced about and took the back trail. It seemed that things were not going so well in Missouri. The bush-whacking and jayhawking of border warfare had created fierce feuds in Nodaway County. Life and property were rather uncertain for those who had taken sides, and it was hard to stay there and not take sides.

We came back to Texas and located in Grayson
County about three miles east of where Denison was
located some four years later. We spent the rest of
the summer building a log house on the prairie. It
had two large rooms with an open hall between, a
shed room behind, and a porch in front.

The one thing I loved to do was ride. It didn't
matter much what it was as long as it was something
with life in it. There were several families that had
boys of my age living around in several miles of us.
On Sundays father made all of us go to Sunday
school. He was a Christian preacher and had ideas
as to how boys should be raised. As soon as Sunday
school was over, we boys struck out for my house
where we rode the calves until the folks got in. Then
we would go to somebody else's house and ride, practice roping and branding. We made life miserable
for the younger calves, but the yearlings held their
own with us.

A cattle trail ran by our place during the late '60s.
It came by Dallas, crossed Red River at Preston
Ferry and went to Baxter Springs, Missouri. During
the late spring and early summer lots of herds came
along this trail. Every time a herd came by, if I
could slip off, I would follow it for miles on my
pony. I suppose some of the drivers thought I was a
nuisance, but some of them kidded me along. One
boss took a liking to me and gave me a pair of spurs.
They were too big for me, but I wouldn't have traded
them for half interest in a bank. Father put a stop
to my wearing them though. He said he wouldn't

have any horse he owned ridden with spurs. So I
had to wear my spurs when I was just walking
around and not riding a horse.

When I was thirteen, a lot of railroad excitement
swept over Grayson County. There was talk of two
railroads coming in our direction, the Missouri, Kansas and Texas, from the north, and the Houston and
Texas Central from the south. A few mass meetings
were held. Real estate agents, merchants, and a few
farmers got up and told what wonders a railroad
would do for a country. It all sounded strange to
me. I had never seen a railroad and could little
imagine what a train looked like. In 1871 the Missouri, Kansas and Texas reached Red River and
started building a bridge across it. About the same
time the Central reached the south boundary of
Grayson County. The M. K. & T. crossed the river
and built on nine miles south where the town of
Denison was laid out and started. The Central passed
Denison and built to Red River where Red River
City was started. The two tracks paralleled each other
for nine miles. The two towns were rivals for a year
or two when Denison so outstripped Red River City
that the few remaining inhabitants abandoned the
place and moved to Denison.

Perhaps the biggest event that had ever taken
place in Grayson County was the arrival of the first
passenger train at Denison. Everybody was there.
The crowd began gathering down at the little plank
depot, not yet finished, hours before the train was
due. But they didn't mind it. It was worth something

just to stand and look down the track. Somebody spied the smoke when the train was fifteen miles away. It was an hour before it got there. I was thrilled when the locomotive with its huge smokestack came in puffing and snorting. As I look back now, I know it must have been a very small engine, but it looked as big as a mountain to me then.

Most of the people in Grayson County had never ridden on a train. A few days later the M. K. & T. ran an excursion train from Denison to Durant, Indian Territory, and back. This was done so as to give the people a chance to ride on a train. I went along, and was so intent on seeing everything that I could not be still. I stuck my head out of the windows, walked up and down the aisles, went from coach to coach, and speculated as to how I could get on top and ride the thing bareback. When we got to Durant, I was out on the steps to be the first one off. I stepped off backwards before the train stopped and hit on my head. This settled me down a little, but on going back I did everything I had done going up except step off backwards. This was my first and last train ride for many years to come.

For several years Denison was the only cattle shipping point in Texas. Herds came from below Gonzales, San Antonio, and Fredericksburg. From April to November there was never a time when there were not a dozen herds in sight of the town waiting to be shipped. The town was always full of drunk and half-drunk cowboys from outfits that had just shipped out. There were more saloons in town than all other places of business put together. Dozens of gambling rackets carried on in the saloons. Down near the railroad track were houses of the prostitutes. For two or three years Denison was beyond doubt the toughest place in Texas. Later there were several other towns as bad, but they all took their cue from Denison.

The place had a strange fascination for boys in their early teens, especially boys who loved to ride wild horses and play at punchin' cattle. Mother was always worried about us, and I expect if she had really known what we were finding out she would have been even more worried.

About this time I secretly traded for an old cap and ball six-shooter. I would slip out and take it to the bottom lands over near the river and practice shooting at trees. I couldn't get much ammunition, but I would practice aiming at trees and posts. I would run by a tree on my horse at full speed and aim without taking sight. I did this so much I got to where I could shoot very well without taking aim.

There were some more boys who lived in the vicinity of the bottom lands. When we would gang up together, my six-shooter raised my prestige considerably. Sometimes I let some of them practice aiming and snapping it. My parents objected to my running with these boys; they said the boys were trifling and no account. Occasionally, I slipped off and went to Denison where I would swagger along the streets with my six-shooter showing. I always felt kinda skittish when I was parading like this, because I never

knew when I might meet father. Father and mother
did find out about the six-shooter in about a year,
and father took it away from me and hid it. I managed to find it, however, and hid it from him.

By the time I was fourteen I was breaking broncs
for all the neighbors. I charged a dollar for riding
a wild horse, but if I couldn't get a dollar, I'd take
fifty cents. Occasionally I would get thrown, but my
riding was getting better all the time. Horses had a
fascination for me and I found the wild ones more
intriguing than the gentle ones.

The worst whipping I ever got was about a horse.
Father had a stallion that he prized very highly. He
would have me ride the stallion on Sundays sometimes just to give him exercise. One Sunday I rode
him to Red River and found the tough gang I was
not supposed to run with. The river was low, and the
water about a hundred yards wide and from a foot
to a foot and a half deep. The boys had a skiff. I tied
a short rope to the horse's tail and started pulling
the boys in the skiff. We went back and forth and
up and down. Then I began to trot the stallion. That
soon got too tame, so I began loping. The afternoon
slipped by before we realized it. When I got home
that evening the stallion could hardly walk. Father
took one good look at him and his face grew stern.
I began to feel dreadfully uncomfortable. But father
didn't say a word until after supper. Then he invited
me to go to the barn with him, and I knew I was in
for it. After it was over, I felt terribly mistreated
and pouted for an hour before I went to bed. I had

thought about running away many times before, and that night I went to sleep determined on it.

CHAPTER II

THE WEGEFARTH EXPEDITION

IN JANUARY, 1873, Conrad Wegefarth, President of the Texas Immigrant Aid and Supply Society, began organizing at Sherman in Grayson County, Texas, a surveying party to locate lands in the Texas Panhandle. The Texas Immigrant Aid and Supply Company planned to bring several hundred German families from Pennsylvania and locate them in the vicinity of what is now Hall, Childress, Collinsworth, and Donley Counties. There was a bill pending in the Legislature at the time to create Wegefarth County from this territory. The bill became a law in May, 1873, but was repealed the following year when the E. J. Davis crowd was turned out of office. The county, as created, was sixty miles square.

The surveying party, when completed, contained one hundred and ten men. Fifty of these were organized into a military company. The men were mounted and equipped with Spencer rifles and Colt 45's. The arms were obtained from the State. Wegefarth and six other members of the Texas Immigrant Aid and Supply Company executed a bond for $2,000, insuring the safe return of the arms to the adjutant general's department. Each man was required to have two good horses. Captain Wegefarth commanded the military company, and was in charge of the entire expedition. L. B. Sieker was First Lieutenant, and his brother, Edward Sieker, was Second Lieutenant. The other sixty men made up the surveying outfit. The military company was to protect the surveyors from the Indians and keep the entire party supplied with fresh meat. The whole outfit was well equipped. The party had eleven large, strong wagons, a good supply of extra horses and mules in case some should be lost, a doctor, and even a small brass band.

I wanted to join the military company, but my parents objected. Mother was dreadfully cut up over the idea even of my thinking of such a thing. The sight of the men riding around the country with their Spencer rifles swinging on their saddles and the handles of their Colts sticking out of their scabbards was too much for me. I resorted to every artifice I could think of to persuade father and mother. In the first week in March the outfit started west. The second day after they left I decided I just had to go, so I began to make plans to leave that night.

Father had a fine horse called Jordan. Jordan was from race stock—brown, trim, and fast. Father used to say that Jordan had more sense than any horse he ever had. That was saying a great deal, for father had had hundreds of horses in his day. Everybody loved Jordan. He seemed one of the family. When I decided to go I felt like I had to take Jordan. My conscience hurt me a little bit, but then I would be leaving the two-year-old colt that father had given me. I concluded I had better not take any luggage, lest my preparations arouse someone's suspicions. I kept Jordan up that night, got a saddle, six-shooter, and spurs ready, and began to wait until everybody went to bed.

It was midnight before I felt I could slip out safely. I slept in the shed room with the other boys, but it wasn't they I feared! a cyclone would hardly wake them up—it was father and mother. Father always slept with one ear cocked, and mother always seemed to have a premonition when something was about to happen. I took an extra pair of pants and tiptoed out. When I had saddled and mounted Jordan, I paused for a moment and looked at the house, and wondered about mother. Then I thought I ought to leave word for the folks about where I was going. So I went to Alf Sewell's place and hollered him up. I told him I was going to join Captain Wegefarth's company, and that it would be useless for them to try to follow me.

Then I hit the road for Gainesville in Cook County. It was forty miles and I got there in the late afternoon to find that Wegefarth's outfit had passed through a few hours before. I pushed on, and found them camped on Elm Creek a few miles west.

I slept on my saddle and saddle-blanket that night, and covered myself with a blanket one of the men let me have. I wasn't used to that kind of sleeping, but I was so tired it didn't matter.

The next morning I approached the captain, and told him I wanted to join his company. He asked me my age, and I told him seventeen. I just lacked one month being sixteen. The captain gave me a quizzical look, and told me his company of fifty mounted men was full. It didn't occur to me to ask if his surveying crew was full. I began to tell the captain how I could ride broncos, and shoot from a horse at full speed. Some of the men standing around suggested that the captain try me out on my riding ability. One of the men of the outfit had a bad horse that had thrown him the day before. I figured they were counting on having a show at my expense; but I had to do something to make an impression, or go back home. So I told them if they had a bronc to trot him out, and if I did not ride him to their satisfaction, I would not ask to join their company. I put my saddle on the horse, caught the cheek of the bridle with my left hand, pulled his head to me, and in a wink was in the saddle. It took the horse a second to figure out what had happened; but when it did dawn on him he began bucking in dead earnest. I encouraged him some more by pulling my old cap and ball six-shooter and firing into the air. The horse was not hard to ride because he jumped straight. There is lots of difference in the way horses buck. Some buck, or pitch, straight; some buck in a zigzag way, and we call that the fence-worm; some do what we call sun-bucking, or sun-fisher, because they turn their sides to the sun, and sometimes their bellies. This last kind is hard to stay on, and generally the rider "hunts leather" or grabs the saddle horn. But I soon saw I could ride this horse, and my satisfaction was great. My chest was sticking out so far I was almost busting the buttons off my shirt before the horse threw his head up and stopped bucking.

The captain was pleased with my performance. He said the company was full and he could not pay me a salary, but he would furnish me an extra horse, a Spencer rifle, and a Colt 45, and I could go along as one of the mounted men. If I had not been where I was expected to maintain a little dignity, I would have started turning handsprings right there.

The outfit was soon on the road toward Montague. There were very few settlers or ranches between Gainesville and Montague, and something like a dozen families made up the population of Montague. Our next destination was Henrietta, about thirty miles to the northwest. Clay County was not organized until two years later, and Henrietta had only three or four log houses when we passed through. Some eight or ten miles northwest of Henrietta was another town of about the same size called Cambridge. Cambridge was the last settlement, and as we continued on northwest we began to realize we were on the frontier. We found deer and turkeys, and the officers told us to "look out a leetle" for Indians. Our next move was for Dan Waggoner's ranch on the Big Wichita River in Wichita County. The night before we got to the ranch we camped on Holiday Creek.

That evening four men were detailed to scout for
fresh meat, and I was one of the four. Soon after
leaving camp we sighted three buffalo, the first I had
ever seen. For days we had been impatient to get to
the buffalo country, and now here we were. The
three men told me to stay where I was while they
undertook to slip up a ravine and get close enough to
take a shot at the buffalo. I didn't like the orders, but
did as they told me. Before the men got in shooting
distance the buffaloes scented them, and started to
run in my direction. They looked as big as covered
wagons, and the closer they got the bigger they
looked. I hesitated for a moment, and then made up
my mind to try and kill one. I left my Spencer rifle
on my saddle, pulled my Colt 45, and headed my
horse toward the buffalo. I had confidence in Jordan's
outrunning everything on earth. I ran up beside the
hindmost buffalo and fired three shots into the big
animal. He slacked his speed and directly tumbled
over. I thought of holding a war dance, but thought
it best to go tell the others about my feat. When I
found them, they had tied their horses in a ravine,
and were cautiously slipping up a hill to shooting
range. They did not know the buffaloes had fled. I
rode up and told them how easy it was to kill a
buffalo. One said, "Kid, quit kidding us." They
wouldn't believe me, and it was only when I had
gone and shown them my kill that they were convinced. Then two men started skinning the animal
while the other and I went to camp to get a wagon
to haul in the meat. They first thought of sending

me alone after the wagon, but they decided the ones
at camp would not believe my story; so one man went
along to vouch for me.

This killing of the first buffalo made a hero of me,
among the officers especially. I was just turning sixteen years, and was rather small to my age; I weighed
about a hundred and twenty pounds. After that I was
always one of four men detailed to do scout work
and keep the outfit supplied with fresh meat.

The next night we camped at Dan Waggoner's
ranch on the Big Wichita. There were some falls in
the river at this place, but I am not sure whether it
was the place where the town of Wichita was later
located or not. The ranch headquarters were nothing
more than a camp made of logs. This was the last
outpost of human habitation towards the northwest.

We travelled up the Big Wichita to the mouth of
Beaver Creek, up Beaver Creek twenty or thirty
miles, and then cut across to Pease River. We proceeded up the Pease for about the same distance, and
then headed northwest to the Prairie Dog Fork of
Red River. It was here we encountered our first vast
herd of buffalo. The herd was slowly drifting north.
Deer and turkeys abounded. The valleys of the
creeks and rivers were covered with prairie dogs.
Every day we saw herds of mustangs.

We had an old frontiersman with us who told us
to look out for a white stallion. It seemed that he
had been encountered and chased in many places before, and that no one had ever been able to make
him break a pace. He could pace faster than any other

horse could run. We all kept a sharp lookout for this noted pacer, but never saw him. I have since read of several story writers who had seen this famous horse. He had been encountered all the way from Devil's River in South Texas to the Kansas line. I have had my doubts that there ever existed such a character in horse flesh.

In the vicinity of where Collinsworth and Wheeler Counties were later located we stopped several days and did some surveying. The chief engineer decided it would be necessary to go to the northeast corner of New Mexico where a monument was supposed to be located and run a line from there in order to establish correctly the boundaries of Wegefarth County.

Just before we came to the Canadian River in what is now Roberts County we came upon another vast herd of buffalo. We camped in sight of the herd for two days, and had an excellent opportunity to observe the movements of the herd. The buffalo were on their way to their summer grazing grounds in Kansas, Nebraska, and the Territories to the north. The animals came in waves, one after another. At times, a section would be two or three hundred yards wide and a mile long. Then there would be a gap of two or three hundred yards in which there would be a few scattered animals; then there would be another wave. Occasionally, as if by a common signal, a section would spread out and begin to graze. At these times the herd would be a mile or two wide with all the buffalo grazing in the same direction. Then, as if by another signal, the herd would come

together again and start trudging northward. During
the two days we watched these shaggy beasts, I heard
the men talking and making guesses as to the number
of buffalo. The lowest estimate was five hundred
thousand, and the others reached from that to one
million. I didn't know anything about estimating the
size of a herd then as I had never seen any big round-
ups. Since then I have seen round-ups containing ten
to sixteen thousand cattle. So in comparison I have
concluded that we saw at least one million buffaloes
pass in two days. I later read in a book by Charles
Siringo where he saw, in 1877, one million buffaloes
at the big lake near where the stock pens at Amarillo
were later located. In 1873 the buffalo hunters had
not yet come into the country, and we little dreamed
as we watched the herd pass that these huge beasts
would soon all fall at the crack of the professional
hunter's gun. The day we broke camp we spent most
of the day passing through this migrating herd.

Just after we crossed the Canadian an Englishman
in the company, Charles Moore, shot and "creased"
a sorrel mustang stallion. He and another scout were
then able to get two lariats on the horse. They
brought him to camp, but did not know what to do
with him. I told Moore I would break the stallion
for half interest in him. Jordan was getting poor,
and I wanted to fix it so he could rest altogether for
awhile. Moore accepted my offer. It was getting late
and I did not have time to ride the animal that night,
so I put a rope on his forefoot and tied it to a bush.
Everybody predicted the horse would be dead or

crippled next morning. When daylight came he was there and not hurt. I decided to top him before breakfast. The whole outfit turned out to see the show. I hit the saddle expecting a hard time of it, but instead the horse bucked a few straights and began to run. I let him go until he began to weaken, and then turned him back to camp. He soon became easy to handle, but I always had to keep him hobbled or staked.

Our next camp was on a little creek which flowed into the Canadian. Here we saw our first recent Indian signs. They had broken camp only a few hours before we arrived. On a big cottonwood tree where the bark had peeled off, an Indian had painted some characters in red. One character, I remember, was an Indian with bow and arrow on horseback chasing a buffalo. There were distinct signs of several *travois*. (A *travois* is made by placing a long pole on each side of a horse, like buggyshafts, and letting the back ends drag on the ground. The back parts are lashed together with short poles. The domestic belongings of the Indians are placed on this makeshift slide, and drug along by the horse.) This party had a considerable number of horses. Our men estimated the number at five hundred.

We camped here for three days, and took every precaution against a surprise attack. The wagons were drawn into a circle and the horses and mules placed inside at night. The number of guards was doubled. The first night we had a big scare. A herd of buffalo stampeded near the camp, and the sound of their

hoofs was like thunder. The roar lasted several
minutes. Everybody knew that the Indians were upon
us. The officers had the bugler to blow a call pre-
paratory for battle. My mettle was up at the moment,
and I was disappointed when nothing came of it. A
little over a year after this an Indian war broke out
in this region and lasted through the fall of 1874 and
the winter of 1874-1875. The United States army
finally rounded up all the Plains tribes and forced
them on the reservations in Indian Territory in 1875.

We moved on, and a few days later some of the
scouts working south of the main party reported finding some old 'dobie ruins. About a year later some
buffalo hunters and a trader from Kansas established
'Dobie Walls near this old ruin. In June, 1874, a
battle took place here. About thirty buffalo hunters
drove off several hundred Indians.

Grass was scarce in the region. Large areas had
been nipped clean by buffaloes. We often had trouble finding sufficient grass for the horses. We kept
moving on to the northwest, stopping over for a day
or so every time we found good water and grass.

We had camped near the northwest corner of the
state when I got into a fight. There was a Frenchman
in the party by the name of Solon DeGraffenreid.
When he was drunk he was always contentious. He
got stewed one day and started picking a quarrel with
me. My general standing in camp demanded that I
do battle with him. I started in, but before I knew
what he was about to do he stabbed me in the left
arm above the elbow with a bowie knife. I pulled my

Colt 45 and struck him over the head, knocking him down. Lieutenant Ed Sieker intervened, and when he saw the blood spurting from my arm, he said, "Kid, why didn't you shoot him?"

The doctor dressed my wound, took a few stitches, and put my arm in a sling. This incident ended my scout work. I had killed more buffaloes than any one else in the outfit. There were others who had killed more deer and turkeys. Such game was too small for me; I always had my eyes cocked for buffalo. I had the best buffalo horse in the party. Jordan was fast and was not afraid of buffaloes. Most horses are afraid and one cannot get them near a buffalo.

After the fight the officers held a courtmartial to determine what to do with DeGraffenreid. They decided that he should wait on me until I got well. He was friendly enough when he wasn't drunk. After he sobered up he seemed to regret the affair more than any one else in camp. For several days he did everything for me.

While I was convalescing I had to stay in camp, and I found camp life exceedingly boring. However, I had plenty of time to witness the usual camp routine. One wagon was loaded with whiskey, tobacco and ammunition. The whiskey and tobacco were sold to the men. I did not use tobacco and had no money to purchase whiskey. The officers, doctor and surveying crew all had wall tents and cook tables. The mounted men had dog tents, two men to each tent. The teamsters slept in or under their wagons. I slept

anywhere I could. We had no tables or special cooks.
Eight men composed a mess that cooked and ate together, rotating the various duties. We ate our meals
cowboy style; and our food consisted of flour bread,
bacon, rice, syrup, coffee, sugar and fresh meat such
as buffalo, deer, turkey and antelope.

About this time some of the mounted men decided
they wanted to go back to civilization. About twenty
of them entered into a mutinous conspiracy. They
argued they had better not make any move until the
Sieker brothers were away on a scout. They had no
respect for Captain Wegefarth, but they were mortal-
ly afraid of the Siekers. The awaited opportunity
soon came. The mutineers appointed a spokesman
whose name was Wright. The men went to Wegefarth and told him they were going to take the back
trail for civilization. Captain Wegefarth made a talk
to the men, and told them they were enlisted in a
military organization, and could not leave until their
term of enlistment had expired. At that, Wright
stepped off a short distance and said, "All of you who
will follow me, come over here." Only five men
went over. Then Wright told Wegefarth they were
going back "if they had to fight the whole damn outfit." The captain told them that if they left, they
could not take any provisions of any kind, and he
put a guard over the commissary. I didn't know anything about the mutiny up to this point, but I can
see why the mutineers didn't want the Sieker boys
there at the time. Had they been there, it would
have meant a fight.

Ever since I had gotten my arm stabbed, I had been having spells of homesickness. It had never bothered me as long as I had been active, but loafing around camp was different. Somehow I was always wondering about what the folks were doing at home, and about mother especially. So when the mutineers got ready to start, I asked the captain if I could go with them. He told me to go. Charley Moore, who had "creased" the mustang, was in ill health and was given permission to leave also. This made eight in all. Wright asked Wegefarth for some salt and flour, but was refused.

We took the back trail with nothing but our horses, saddles, and arms. The captain first thought of taking our arms away from us, but changed his mind. He thought that we might meet Indians on the way. He let us take the arms on condition we would turn them in at Fort Richardson at Jacksboro when we got back. We went back the same trail we had made going up. It was easy to follow, for eleven heavy wagons leave a pretty good road. We ate buffalo meat without salt or bread. We soon found that such a fare did not agree with us, for we all took dysentery. At first we broiled the meat on sticks over coals, but later got to covering it with ashes and roasting it. We finally got to broiling liver until it was dry and hard. This seemed to relieve us of our complaint.

On the trip I learned that the six men were criminals of the worst type. They spent most of the time telling of their crimes. Some of them had gun-shot wounds that were barely healed up. They got a peculiar satisfaction out of showing these to each other. Charley Moore was all right. He and I threw in together and became fast friends.

On the ninth day we got to Waggoner's camp on the Big Wichita. The cook had just killed a man that morning, but he was as calm and collected as if nothing had happened and cooked us a good meal. He gave us bread, molasses, beef, and coffee. We went easy on the beef, but bore down heavy on the bread, molasses, and coffee.

On the way to Henrietta we came upon a prairie fire. It was not a large one, so we decided to stop and put it out. We left one man holding the horses while the rest of us started fighting fire on foot. We used our heavy army overcoats to swipe it out. The man holding the horses let them get away, and when we caught them my Spencer rifle was gone. I was glad of it and did not go to any trouble to find it. These rifles were designed for a saddle gun, but were too heavy for that purpose. They used a centerfire cartridge, the first I ever saw.

When we got to Henrietta we got another good meal of meat, cornbread, and coffee. Our next stop was at Montague. Our victuals were improving; here we got hot biscuits, ham, eggs, molasses and coffee.

At Montague we separated into three groups. No one went to the trouble of turning his arms in at Fort Richardson. Four of the outlaws left for Indian Territory, two of them started to Denison, and Moore and I pulled out for Fort Worth. I left Moore at Fort Worth and went on to Weston, Collin County, where my father had lived before 1867. After we had gotten back into the settlements my homesickness had abated, and I decided not to go home for awhile.

CHAPTER III

ESTABLISHING A RANCH IN
C— COUNTY

When I got to Weston I wrote to father, the first time since I left home. I wanted to let them know I was all right, and had not been scalped by the Indians. I was staying around with old neighbors and friends while waiting to hear from home. My arm was still bothering me. The wound had proud flesh in it and was healing slowly. When it finally did heal it left a deep scar about the size of a quarter, and that arm has bothered me off and on ever since.

In August, 1873, while I was still waiting, I met an ambitious cowman whom, for perfectly obvious reasons, I will call Mr. X. Mr. X. had acquired a small herd of cattle in Collin County and was intending to start a ranch in C— County. I hired to Mr. X. to help drive the herd to C— County. At the time the herd pulled out, Mr. X. started four wagons loaded with dry goods to Palo Pinto, where he expected to trade the merchandise for more cattle to take to his C— County ranch. Just before the herd I was with reached Mr. X.'s range on the W—

River, Charles Grimes and I were ordered to cut across the country and join the wagons on the way to Palo Pinto. We overtook the outfit late the next day. The second day after we joined this party, Jim Brown and I were scouting along ahead of the wagons, and ran across a big black bear and her two half-grown cubs. We started after them, and the old one took the lead and was soon out of sight. We had no trouble keeping up with the cubs. We debated whether to shoot them, or rope and take them in alive. Roping appealed to us the more. We made two or three passes at them with our lariats. When we landed the loops on their necks, the cubs certainly did cut a shine for a spell. We tried leading them, but discovered that didn't go. Then we tried driving, and found that worked almost too well. The cubs were strong, and kept the ropes taut for three or four miles to the place where we were to camp. That night we tied the cubs to a wagon wheel. The next morning mine was gone. Jim took his bear to Fort Richardson at Jacksboro, and traded him for a gallon of whiskey. Of all the whiskey I have ever tasted, that gallon was the hardest. One swallow was enough for me. It was not unusual during the 70's and 80's for one to rope a bear. Later, in 1883, some cowboys roped a black bear north of Yellow House Canyon some ten miles east of where Lubbock is now located. I was just across the Canyon when it happened. The same year a cowboy roped a bear in the vicinity of Gail in Borden County.

When we got to Palo Pinto the boss traded the
dry goods to Scott and Warren for cattle. The cattle
had to be gathered and branded. So we established
our camp on Ironi Creek about two miles from Palo
Pinto. Scott and Warren's camp was on the other side
of the creek. The creek was very rough and could
only be crossed in a few places. I suppose they placed
the camps on opposite sides of the creek so the horses
would not mix.

One bright, moonlight night a few days after they
camped there, Comanche Indians attacked Scott and
Warren's camp. We heard a big rumpus over there,
the Indians whooping, and the cowboys firing with
their six-shooters. There were six cowboys in camp,
and they were making the bombardment sound
mighty interesting. Our boss ordered all our outfit to
the fight, but by the time we got across the creek
the battle was over. We fired our guns as we rushed
along just to let the boys on the other side know
we were coming. None of the Scott and Warren men
were hurt, but they evidently got an Indian. The next
morning we found where one had fallen and there
was a pool of blood on the ground. The other Indians
had evidently carried the wounded or dead one off,
as was their custom. The Indians used bows and arrows. There were several arrows sticking in the side
of the wagon and in the ground close by. Another
boy and I found a bow and a quiver full of arrows
about a hundred yards from the camp. We supposed
the wounded Indian had dropped them. I took the
bow and some of the arrows, and the other boy got

the quiver and the rest of the arrows. The cook of the Scott and Warren outfit was so scared that he ran all the way to Palo Pinto and gave the alarm. He said the Indians were massacring all the boys at the camp. The people in the town were so alarmed they didn't sleep any that night. When we got back to camp our cook was missing. He had taken to the brush. He came slipping in after awhile, and wanted to know how many of the boys were killed.

It took us about two weeks to get the cattle rounded up. Ordinarily, three or four days would have been sufficient time to gather a herd of that size, but these cattle were as wild as mustangs, and the country was hard to work. The thick cedar brush and numerous hills and ravines made it necessary for the boys to work close together. When we jumped one of those wild creatures it took about two punchers to head her the way we wanted to go.

I was sent up to Palo Pinto one day and got there just in time to witness a fight. One of the combatants was a red-headed Irishman whose name was Bell, and the other was a fellow with a local reputation as a bad man. The fight started in a saloon and ended in the street. The bad man was larger than Bell and soon had Bell down. He was trying to get Bell's pistol. Bell managed to wrench around and take three shots at the other's head, barely missing it each time by a hair's breadth. Nobody around seemed to care about interfering. There might have been a killing had the sheriff not finally arrived on the scene and stopped the fight.

When we got our herd gathered and branded we
started to the C— County ranch. One night we
camped in the Keechi Valley, near the south line of
Jack County. The next morning about daylight a
man, bare-headed and blear-eyed, came running into
our camp. He was scared so he could scarcely talk.
He said that Indians were at the moment massacring a man and a boy just over the ridge about a mile
and a half away. Our boss took five men and started
to the place indicated by the man, on a dead run.
When they got there they found the man and boy
scalped, and the Indians gone.

The murdered man's name was Walker, and the
boy was his son. The man who came to our camp was
Steve Martimer. It seemed that the three had been
traveling in a wagon drawn by oxen. They had broken
camp before daylight, and had just started on the
road when the Indians swooped down on them. Steve
jumped off the wagon on the far side and took down
a small creek. The Indians evidently did not see him,
and he got away, and soon ran into us.

This affair delayed us for a day and night. Our
boss sent a man to the nearest ranch house, several
miles away, to give the alarm about the Indians and
tell about the murder. The four of us who had been
left in charge of the herd that morning rode over
later in the day to look at the dead men. It was a
ghastly sight. They had been shot with arrows. Both
had been scalped and had a small rim of hair left on
their necks. The boy, who was about sixteen, had
one hand cut off at the knuckles; otherwise, the

bodies were not mutilated. We left the bodies in charge of neighboring ranchmen who came in after the report had been spread around.

We had been having trouble with the cattle. It had been storming and we had scarcely slept at all for two nights. We were dead on our feet and were glad to get a little sleep that night.

As we proceeded northward our outfit engaged in cattle stealing in wholesale fashion. The brazenness displayed by our boss in taking other people's cattle has been equaled in recent times only by some of the doings of Chicago gangsters. The boss had two men scouting on each side of the trail. These men rode through the range cattle on either side of the trail, and cut the best cows and all the mavericks they could find into the herd. They had a list of brands that belonged in Palo Pinto and Jack Counties. From the best I could make out these were brands belonging to ranchmen whom Mr. X. did not dare to steal from. Mr. X. claimed he had a right to gather certain brands, but I noticed we always put his brand and earmark on all the cattle brought in. His earmark was "grub" one and "sharp" the other, thus ⟨▷◁⟩ At that time I did not know what this mark indicated. In later years I discovered that when you saw a man "grubbing" and "sharping," you could put it down he was a thief, and nine times out of ten you would be right. I came to doubt the honesty of any man who "grubbed" the ears of his cattle.

We moved the herd slowly and laid over every other day. The four men doing the rustling brought

in ten to fifty head every day we laid up. One of
the boys on night herd told me that bunches of cattle
were frequently driven into the herd at night. In all,
the outfit stole nearly a thousand cattle on this drive.
I have later had cause to believe that a good many
big cattlemen who became rich and their families re-
spected got their start this way.

Another boy and I did the wrangling on this
drive. There were Indians in the country, and the
boss was afraid they would drive off the horses. So
to foil the Indians, the other boy and I took the
remuda off a mile or two from camp and guarded
them at night; one of us would sleep while the other
watched the horses.

Finally, we arrived at Mr. X.'s range on the
W— River. There were only three other cow outfits in C— County at the time. The T. J. A. outfit was
located on a creek in the southern part of the county.
The S. W. outfit was on the W— River below Mr.
X.'s range. There was another outfit whose name I
have forgotten on Y— River at the mouth of the
W— River. Our headquarters consisted of the chuck
wagons and a tent. We had no corrals of any kind.

About a month later Mr. X.'s uncle arrived from
Z— County with a herd of three thousand long-
horn steers, three years old and up. After the cattle
were counted and turned on the range, Mr. X.'s
uncle sent his outfit, mostly Mexicans, back to
Z— County. The uncle remained with us a couple
of months.

Camp life with Mr. X.'s outfit during the fall and winter was strenuous. Our range was about ten miles square, and, fortunately, there were no other cattle near the boundary. The longhorns were in a strange country and were not used to cold weather, especially snow. Every norther caused them to drift badly. All of the punchers, ten besides the cook, had to be up, through with breakfast, and on our cayuses by daylight, rain or snow. The worse the weather the farther we had to go in order to get outside the cattle that were sure to be drifting south.

Indians raided through the country almost every light-of-the-moon. We were not much afraid of their attacking the camp at night. Indians were leery of a bunch of cow punchers who slept with a revolver or two by their sides and both ears cocked. But we were afraid they would get the horses. So for about one week out of every four we had to drive the *remuda* off to some unlikely place at a distance from the camp and guard them all night. Two men took the horses out each night; one guarded until midnight while the other slept, and then they traded. We were always glad when the full moon was over and standing horse guard was done.

Mr. X.'s uncle was a great hunter. As long as he stayed with us he kept the outfit supplied with deer and turkey, and after he left the rest of us took turns at the job. The turkeys were fat on pecans. They swallowed the pecans whole and the juices of the craw melted the hulls. I have taken a double handful of pecans from the craw of one turkey. The hulls

would be in all stages, some soft and some hard.
The nut seemed to have a better flavor in the soft
stage. When spring came the turkeys took to eating
wild onions, and the meat became so strongly flavored
with onions we had to quit eating them until the
young ones got large enough to eat. They ate onions
too, but their meat was not so highly flavored.

Turkeys roosted in the trees along the streams.
They came into the roosts between sundown and
dusk. That sputtering, clucking noise that turkeys
make could be heard most anywhere along the W—
River late every evening. One evening as another
puncher and I were coming into camp we saw about
thirty turkeys coming into roost, but were still over
a mile from timber. We took after them on our
horses, and they flew about three hundred yards.
When they lit on the ground we were close to them.
They flew again but not so far. When they lit the
second time they could not leave the ground any
more. Then we drove the turkeys to camp, and the
boys killed them with sticks. This was one of the
biggest turkey killings I ever took part in. If these
turkeys had not been so excessively fat they could
have flown to the timber.

After Mr. X.'s uncle had been there about two
months he sold the three thousand steers to Mr. X.
and went back to Z— County. Along with the
steers he had brought one hundred and fifty Spanish
horses which he also sold to Mr. X. Fifty of these
horses were unbroken. Mr. X. wanted some one to
break them. I told him I would take the job for five

dollars a month extra. I was already getting twenty-five dollars a month. He agreed and gave me three months to get the breaking done. It was a hard job. I had to do all my regular work and average breaking a horse in less than two days. Inasmuch as one horse had to be ridden and handled daily for a period of three to ten days, depending on how wild he was, I had to ride several bucking horses everyday. Some of them were comparatively easy to ride and some were veritable devils. When I got my saddle on one especially bad, I rode him just as far as he could go. The next time his gusto was not so manifest. Mr. X. got this bunch of horses broke for thirty cents apiece. The usual difference in the price of a broke horse and an unbroke one was five dollars. Before I got through with the job I had my fill of riding bucking horses. After that experience I rode one occasionally, but I never had any desire to ride them in wholesale quantities.

During the winter about a hundred of our cattle wandered off. We had an idea that they had gone into the Big W— country. The boss told three other punchers and myself to pack a horse with chuck and bed rolls and go find the cattle, and not to come back until we had found them. The weather was dreadfully cold. About thirty miles from the ranch we located a temporary camp, and next morning started out in pairs to look for the cattle. My partner and I rode about five miles, and decided to separate. We agreed to meet again at a certain point. I had not gone far when I ran across several buffaloes. I gave chase and got pretty close to one. My horse was afraid and kept slinging his head about, and trying to head off another way. I finally maneuvered up within pistol range. I was slightly behind the buffalo and to his right, and had to fire at a cross angle across my horse's head. Just as I fired, my horse gave a wild swing and caught the bullet right in the top of the head. The horse never knew what hit him. We rolled over together, but somehow I got up unhurt. There I was, afoot, in an Indian country, five miles from camp, with a saddle, saddle blanket, six-shooter, and cartridge belt. I got all these things on my back and started hoofing it back to camp. I had not gone far when my partner topped a hill a couple of miles away and saw me. We put my luggage on his horse and we both footed it back to camp. A few days later we found the cattle. When we got back to the ranch I told the boss my horse had fallen and broken his neck. I didn't like to do that, but I knew he would charge me twice the value of the horse and take it out of my wages. He was so pleased over our finding the cattle that he didn't say much about the horse.

We saw lots of coyotes that winter. They were mostly in bunches of twenty-five or thirty. Coyotes are cowardly creatures. They never attack anything unless they have every advantage and are mighty sure of themselves. They won't take chances like a lobo will. They lived for the most part on small game such as rabbits, turkeys, small antelope and deer. If they could find a small calf with its mother away they would pounce on it. Occasionally, if they got hungry enough and if the pack were large enough, they would attack a grown cow. Instead of snapping at the ham strings in the back legs like lobos did, they grabbed the tail. We found lots of cows that winter with their tails bitten off. Coyotes are mighty shy. In later years, when we were driving on the trail, we sometimes killed a beef when we camped at night. We always drove the animal to be slaughtered up close to the wagon so we wouldn't have to carry the beef so far. During the night coyotes would slip up within fifteen feet of where men were sleeping to get the head and entrails of the carcass. Many times I have raised up on my elbow and killed a coyote with my six-shooter.

Mr. X. was a tough man. He kept whiskey in camp by the barrel, together with a supply of tobacco, ammunition, and cheap clothing suitable for cow punchers. He sold these articles to the boys at a high price. He would play cards with the punchers for a quart of whiskey or anything else the boys wanted, and he nearly always won. In this way he managed to fleece the punchers out of most of the wages they had coming. During the winter two men came to camp and hired to Mr. X. One was fleshy, and we called him "Fatty." The other was slim and bony, and we called him "Bones." If they had any other names we never did know what they were. They were sharp with the cards, and got to playing seven-up and poker with Mr. X. They soon cleaned him of all the money he had as well as a couple of horses. The boss was a bad loser. When he lost his third horse, he put on a regular two-gun gambling house display. If "Fatty" and "Bones" had bucked up, we would have had a killing. As it was, though, "Fatty" and "Bones" slipped out and left for parts unknown.

The cook's name was "Soggy." He was a dirty, filthy fellow. He never washed his hands (or any of the rest of his person for that matter) unless he got them wet by accident when he was mucking out the pots and pans. He chewed tobacco, and the juice had a way of running down his chin from the corners of his mouth. I often saw him spatter ambeer in the sourdough, but cow punchers were not very finicky about their victuals in those days. Soggy was in cahoots with the boss, and kept an eagle eye on the wagon containing the merchandise—clothing, ammunition, tobacco and whiskey. It was his business to sell these commodities and charge them against our "time."

Mr. X. furnished the outfit with flour, beans, coffee, molasses, salt, and soda, but we had to rustle our meat. That was easy to do as game was plentiful. Occasionally we took a notion for buffalo. A couple of us would take a pack horse and go over into W— or A— Counties, as few buffalo ever came into C— County. If we wanted beef, we had orders to kill a stray. Any hand who would have killed an animal with Mr. X.'s brand on it would have gotten fired.

There were no slickers in those days; at least, if there were, I had never heard of them. The punchers, if they could, procured a blue army overcoat with a cape attached to keep the rain off. The material in these coats was so tightly woven they would turn the hardest rain. They were very hard to get. They could not be purchased in a legitimate fashion at all. One had to barter for them clandestinely from the soldiers stationed at the various army posts. The soldiers would tell their commanding officer they had lost their coats and get new ones issued. The boys in our outfit who were lucky enough to have coats got them from the negro soldiers at Fort Richardson. The usual price of a coat was a quart of whiskey. The punchers who had no coats would cut a cross in the middle of a blanket and put their heads through this slit. Practically all the blankets in the outfit had a U. S. on them and were procured in the same way as the overcoats.

Each of us wore a large handkerchief, usually red, around our necks. We used this for drying our faces after washing, for wiping the sweat from our faces in hot weather, for covering our ears in cold weather, and for blindfolding our horses when occasion demanded it. We never got a bath, shave or hair cut until we went to town, which was once or twice a year. When we did go in our beards were two to four inches long and our hair was down to our shoulders. Occasionally we had a swim, if we could find a hole deep enough. Once in a while we made an effort to wash our clothes, but it didn't amount to much, because we washed them in muddy creek water, and we never had any soap. We usually stayed in the water while our clothes were drying on bushes.

I left Mr. X.'s outfit in August, 1874. A short time after I left, he killed a man. It was only a starter for him though, as I understood he marked up several notches on his gun after that. I had been away from home seventeen months and decided I wanted to see the folks. They were awfully glad to see me. For several days after I got home, the folks and the neighbors who came in to see me "oh'ed" and "ah'ed" about how much I had grown and filled out. I gave the boys in the community several thrills by showing them the scar in my left arm.

I had left a girl down in the timber not far from home. I guess I must have been in love with her, for I had spent many an hour thinking about her while I had been away. Anyway, I didn't lose any time in getting over to see her the first Sunday after I got home. She had two sisters and six brothers ranging from ten to twenty years of age.

There were some more visitors, and everybody couldn't eat at the first table. One of the girls was kept busy shooing the flies off the table with a long willow branch which she waved back and forth. The younger boys who had to wait were hanging around the table. One of them was right behind me with his foot on the round of my chair. We got through eating chicken, gravy and the like, and came to the trimmings. Now, I was just seventeen months behind on pie and cake, so I asked for a second piece of pie. I suppose my girl's brothers were kinda behind on pie too, because the brat holding on to my chair said in a stage whisper that everybody heard, "Eat meat, confound you!"

I suppose I turned crimson behind my ears, but it didn't embarrass me nearly as much as it did the girls. I had been short on pie and cake and long on meat; I had the pie on my plate, and I did not offer to give it up. After I recovered myself, I felt sorry for my girl. She looked as if she wanted to go through a knot hole in the floor.

CHAPTER IV

A THREE-MAN TRAIL OUTFIT

In September, 1874, I hired to George B. Loving. Loving at that time was devoting all of his time to buying cattle in Jack and Wise Counties, driving them to Denison, and shipping to Chicago to market. He bought the cattle in large bunches and small bunches, mostly small. He had a rounding-up outfit which did nothing but go around and gather these cattle. Then he had twelve three-men trail outfits which received the cattle from the rounding-up outfit and drove them to Denison.

The equipment for a three-man outfit was carried on a pack horse, or mule. It consisted of one pair of blankets for each man, a small frying pan, a butcher knife, a coffee pot, a coffee grinder, and a small cooking oven. Sometimes we did not have an oven and just cooked the bread by twisting the dough on a stick and holding it over a fire. Our provisions consisted of half a sack of flour, a strip of bacon, several pounds of parched coffee, salt, black pepper, and baking powder. We mixed the biscuits in the flour sack. We kept a small piece of sourdough in the top of the sack. We would roll the top of the flour sack down, add baking powder, salt, and water to the sour dough and mix a batch of biscuits, always leaving some dough to sour for next time. Occasionally we would pass a ranch or farm house and get the wife to bake us a batch of biscuits. We always furnished the material. Sometimes she would not charge us anything for the baking, but if she did, the customary price was ten cents a dozen.

We usually drove about three hundred head at a time. That constituted a train load. A car held from twenty-six to thirty head, and a train contained from ten to twelve cars. Locomotives were small at that time, and road grades were much steeper than later.

A three-man outfit was a sort of combination between a drive and a drift. Two men did most of the work. They maneuvered all around the herd. Instead of stringing the herd out, they drove the cattle in a bunch. The pack horse was herded along with the cattle. The boss was usually on ahead looking for water, selecting a camping place, or getting some housewife to cook some biscuits. Guard duty at night was divided into three shifts of about two and a half hours each. A three-man outfit could make better time than a larger outfit because it didn't take so long to water and fill up.

While working for Loving I saw several one-man outfits. A one-man herd usually numbered about one hundred and fifty. A Mr. Kimberlin went alone from Jack County to Denison for three or four years. He would employ a couple of cowboys for two days to help him break the cattle to the trail. He had a pack

horse to carry his camping equipment. He drifted the
cattle during the day and slept during the night.
When cattle got up from the bed ground in the night,
they always started bawling. The driver always slept
with both ears open. When the bawling started, he
would get up and walk around the herd until the
cattle bedded down again. Cattle always get up about
midnight, mill around a little, and then bed down
again. Grass and water were usually plentiful on the
trails from Palo Pinto, Jack, and Wise Counties to
Denison, and most any herd is easy to manage when
it is full of grass and water.

I started to work for Loving near the end of the
driving season in 1874, and made only three trips
that fall. Pat Sweeney was the boss, and Charley
Sibley and I were the crew. On our third trip we had
a little catastrophe. Our pack animal was a mule. In
the late afternoon just as we were going down Jim
Ned Mountain in Jack County the pack slipped to
one side a little bit so that the coffee pot got under
the mule's belly. We always carried the butcher knife
in the coffee pot with the handle down. It was a little
too long, so we cut a slit in the coffee pot lid, and let
a half inch of the end of the blade stick out through
the slit. When the point of the butcher knife got to
jabbing the mule's belly, he began to pitch. The more
he pitched, the more the knife jabbed him.

Before we could stop him, he had scattered our
grub over about a half acre. He was not hurt much;
the skin was cut in several places, but the wounds
were not deep. The bad part of it was it was our

first day out and we didn't have a thing left to eat.
We were hungry the most of that trip. We managed
to get a little grub from a few other outfits we passed,
and from the few ranch houses along the way.

When we laid off for winter, I went home and
stayed until June, 1875. Then I made five more
drives for Loving during that summer and fall.
Sweeney, Sibley and I made up our outfit again. On
the last drive of the fall we had another calamity
to happen to our grub supply. We were about eight
miles from Gainesville when a severe rainstorm began and lasted all night. We did not get any supper
and we had to stay up all night with the cattle. The
next morning we found our flour and coffee water-
soaked. Then we decided to broil some bacon, but
found our matches were wet. Sweeney gave Charley
some money and sent him to Gainesville to get some
provisions. Sweeney and I started on with the herd.
About noon we saw Charley coming back. We threw
the cattle off the trail and got ready for a big feed,
as we had not eaten anything for twenty-four hours.

Charley came up and said, "Here she is, boys."
"She" turned out to be a watermelon and a pint of
whiskey. Sweeney didn't say anything for a moment.
I have never been able to figure out whether it was
because he could not think of words strong enough
to express himself just then, or whether it was because he thought of so many forceful expressions that
they all got jammed in his throat. But when he did
get going, he got exceedingly eloquent. When he
managed to cool down a little, he left Charley to

mind the herd while he and I rode to Gainesville
to get a square meal.

After we got to Denison, I was in a barber shop
when one of Loving's other bosses came in to get a
general cleanup. He was slim, rawboned, and had a
prominent Roman nose. He looked pretty woolly, as
it had been about thirty days since he had been in
a barber shop. When the barber got a good lather on
Parker's face, one of the local town bullies came in
and said to the barber, "How long is it going to take
you to finish shaving that damn corpse?" Parker
raised up in the chair, drew his six-shooter, and took
a shot at the fellow just as he went out of the door.
After that, everybody was mighty polite to Mr.
Parker every time he went in to get a shave.

I spent the winter of 1875-1876 at home in Grayson County. In the spring of 1876, Mr. Alf Sewell,
a neighbor to my father, sold his farm with the view
of migrating to Little Lost Valley in Jack County.
He employed me to drive his little herd of cattle,
about one hundred and fifty head in all. Mr. Sewell
delegated his twelve-year-old boy to help me while
he and his wife followed behind us with a couple
of two-horse wagons loaded with moving plunder.
He told me to take the lead and he would camp
where and whenever I said. This was the first time
I ever bossed a herd, and although I did practically
all the work, I just couldn't get over the feeling that
I was the boss. The boy was some help to me during
the day, but I did all the night guarding. In the
daytime we were a two-man outfit, and at night a

one-man outfit. After bedding the cattle down at night, I would stake my horse near the herd, and lie down near the cattle. If the cattle would get restless and start moving off, I would drive them back on foot. A few times I did not wake soon enough and the cattle became scattered. On such occasions I would mount my horse and drive them back to the bed ground.

When we arrived in Little Lost Valley we made a camp, and a short time later Mr. Sewell sent the boy and me to Fort Worth for lumber and put me to drive the oxen. The boy was to follow behind me with a two-horse wagon. When we arrived at Fort Worth we put up at the wagon-yard on Main Street and went uptown to see the lumberman. He told me that he did not have all the lumber on my bill in stock, but he had a carload of lumber coming in the next day when the first freight on the Texas and Pacific would arrive at Fort Worth. There was nothing to do but to wait, and we were more than glad to do that. Fort Worth was a typical frontier cow-town at that time. The main Kansas cattle trail ran close by and crossed the river just west of where the courthouse is now located. The town was full of cowboys, saloons, and all the other things that go with punchers and whiskey. I wanted to cut loose and do all the things done by a "cowboy come to town," but I had the kid with me, and I kinda felt responsible for him.

That night we cooked our own supper, and slept on the floor of the bunk house at the wagon-yard.

The next morning we went down to see the train
come in. Nearly everybody in town and for miles
around was down by the railroad. Some were in
wagons, some in buggies, some were horseback, and a
lot more were hoofing it like we were. The last mile
or so of the railroad was not on a dump at all, but
the crossties were laid on the turf. I suppose they
did this because they were under contract to have a
train in town by a certain time. We had not been
down there long when we saw smoke down the track.
Everybody gave a big yell. After awhile the train
came pulling in—very slowly because the turf underneath the crossties was giving pretty badly. The locomotive was hot and panting and seemed exhausted.
It was pulling twelve or fifteen freight cars. The
crowd gave another yell as the train pulled in and
stopped.

It was next day before we got our wagons loaded
and headed west. The weather was hot and the oxen
contrary. The flies nearly drove them crazy, and
every time we passed some trees those pesky oxen
would hike for the shade. It didn't do much good to
try to stop them, for when an ox gets his head set,
there is just one way to stop him, and that is to kill
him. I felt like murdering the whole bunch plenty
of times. They got the wagon in all kinds of jack-
pots, and almost turned it over several times.

To make matters worse, the boy got sick, and became unable to drive his team. I made a bed for him
on his wagon, tied his team on behind my ox wagon,
and drove the rest of the way home. Before I got

back to Sewell's place I vowed I would never start out with another ox outfit as long as I lived. I helped Mr. Sewell build his house, and left for home.

When I got to Denison I got a job for the fall and winter with a butcher by the name of John C. Denney. My wages were ten dollars a month and board. However, the dignity of my position made up for what I didn't get in wages. I was the purchasing agent for the firm. I went around the country buying fat cattle, sheep, and hogs for the meat market. I had a big time that winter. While going about the country I heard about all the parties and dances for miles around. I always saw to it that my official duties made it necessary for me to stay in the vicinity of the party or dance the night that it took place.

During the fall Denney persuaded me to ride a three-year-old steer on the main street in Denison. He advertised that at two o'clock of a certain afternoon, the buffalo hunter, scout, cow-puncher, and bronc buster, Rollie Burns, would ride a wild steer on Main Street. At the time set I was there with the steer. The street was lined with people. Farmers had come in for miles around to see the exhibition. Denison was no longer the wild, rollicking place it had been a few years before. Fort Worth and Fort Griffin in Shackelford County had eclipsed Denison's reputation. So the spectacle of a puncher riding a wild steer down Main Street would be a reminiscence of the old days, and the people turned out to see it. The steer did a good job of bucking for a block or so, and then, raising his head, started running down the middle of the street. Mr. Denney ran along side of us on his horse, roped the steer, and I got off.

The job of riding over the countryside and looking at pigs finally got old to me, and when spring (1877) came I was fired with a desire to go to Jack County and get a job on a ranch. When I got to Jack County I found jobs scare in that vicinity. At Jacksboro I met Major Carnes, a beef buyer. He had a small outfit and was going to Fort Griffin to look for some cattle to buy. He invited me to go along with him. When we got to Fort Griffin he didn't find any beeves to purchase. We loafed around the place for awhile and found life there fast and wild.

At the time Fort Griffin was the principal supply base for the buffalo hunters for two hundred miles to the west. A new cattle trail to Dodge City, Kansas, had just been started by the place, and Fort Griffin was the last point where trail outfits could get supplies until they got to Kansas.

On a hill to the south was the fort where soldiers were stationed. In the valley north of the fort was the town called the "Flats." The town was made up of two or three general supply stores, a dozen saloons, several restaurants, small dives, and houses of lewd women. The houses for the most part were pickets with flat roofs made of poles and dirt. Beyond the town was the camp of the Tonkaway Indians. The "Flats" were alive and hustling during the day. Freighters were unloading wagons, trail outfits were taking on supplies, the wagons of buffalo hunters were loading out, and hide freighters were getting ready to start to Fort Worth. Alongside this busy element was another, half drunk, boisterous, and bent on raising hell. Soldiers, Tonks, hunters, punchers from passing trail outfits, adventurers and desperadoes all mingled together and played the saloons and gambling rackets. Robbery was frequently perpetrated in broad daylight, and at night the "Flats" was a din of ribaldry, lewd women, designing gamblers, and drunken thieves.

Major Carnes heard of an old army friend of his who had a buffalo camp about one hundred and fifty miles to the northwest. After sampling the gay life of the "Flats" a few days, the Major decided to pay his friend a visit out in the buffalo country. He left one man at Fort Griffin (he was glad to stay) with the horses and took two others and myself with him. As we travelled northwest we saw several small herds of buffalo, but they were not nearly as plentiful as I had seen them in the Panhandle in 1873, before the slaughter began. We found the camp of the Major's friend on Catfish Creek just below the caprock of the Plains. As we approached the Caprock from the east, I thought it was a long, flat mountain.

This was the first buffalo hunter's camp I had ever seen. The smell about the place was putrid. I'll never forget the aroma that greeted us as we rode up. Gas masks had not been invented in those days, but if they had been, and if I had had one, I would have worn it the whole time I was there. About an acre was covered with hides stretched over the ground drying.

Some of the hides had the flesh side up and some had the hair side up. I noticed that they turned the hides over every two or three days. When the hides were dry they stacked them in piles and tied them into huge bales ready to be hauled to Fort Worth or Fort Griffin. A scaffold built of cottonwood and mesquite poles was used to dry and cure the tongues, humps and backstrips. We could stand in camp and tell exactly where killings, or stands, had been made in the various directions by the buzzards. Thousands of buzzards circled lazily in the air above the carcasses. I am told that buzzards were never fatter than during the time of the buffalo slaughter.

Within a year the buffaloes were almost completely exterminated. The sequel to the hide industry was the bone industry. After the Texas and Pacific built west from Fort Worth in 1880 and 1881, people discovered that buffalo bones had a value. Thousands of persons went bone gathering. Bones were shipped by the car load and train load from Colorado, Sweetwater and Abilene. In 1882 I saw a pile of bones a quarter of a mile long and ten feet high alongside the railroad track at Colorado City.

After staying at the buffalo camp for a few days, we returned to Jacksboro by way of Fort Griffin. Major bought about three hundred beeves, and we drove the herd to Denison where we loaded the steers on the train for Chicago. I spent the rest of that year and the winter of 1877-1878 at home.

CHAPTER V

ALMOST A RANGER

In the spring of 1878, Barney Thomas, who lived in the same neighborhood as my father in Grayson County, wanted to drive a herd of two hundred yearlings to Kimble County. Mr. Thomas employed me to drive the cattle. He sent his twelve-year-old grandson along with me. We had two horses apiece and a pack horse. Mr. Thomas was going through in a hack, but started us on ahead, saying he would overtake us in a day or two. It was ten days before he caught us. He probably would not have overtaken us that soon had we not been held up at the San Saba River. That stream was bank-full, and we were waiting for it to run down. Mr. Thomas stayed with us until we got across the river; then, he told me that we were getting along so well that he would go on and wait for us at Junction City, the county seat of Kimble County. We reached Junction on schedule time without any mishap at all. I herded the cattle for about a month for Mr. Thomas, and then he sold them. That left me without a job.

I heard of a camp of Texas Rangers about twelve miles up the North Llano River at the mouth of

Bear Creek. It occurred to me that I might join the Rangers. I had two good horses and a Colt 45. The more I thought of the idea, the more it intrigued me. I went up to the camp to see what the situation was. To my surprise I found both Sieker brothers, L. B., and Ed, there as lieutenants in the Ranger service. I had not seen or heard of them since I left Captain Wegefarth's Company in the northwest part of the State in 1873. They both recognized me at once, and gave me a hearty welcome. I told them I wanted to join the Rangers. They said that Captain Roberts was away just then, but that they would recommend me when he returned. I waited at the camp until the captain came in. When he arrived I had a talk with him, and he promised to take me in his company the first vacancy that occurred.

The fall and winter, while I was waiting for the vacancy, I spent most of the time on the chuck line. I was at the Ranger camp a lot. The rest of the time I was making the rounds of the various cow oufits in the country trying to get a job. Nobody seemed to need a hand at that time of year. They always asked me to stay around a few days and rest up, and that I was mighty glad to do, because I was getting low on funds.

I had to get my horse shod, and that cost a couple of dollars. Horses need shoes a lot worse in some sections of the country than in others. Where a person had a number of horses in his string so he did not use any one horse very much and in smooth range, it was usually not necessary to have the horses shod at all.

On sandy ranges, horses were never shod, but occasionally the hoofs and the bottom parts of the feet were trimmed to evenness. In dry, hard ranges, horses were usually shod in front, and had their rear feet trimmed. While in a rocky, hilly country it was necessary to keep riding horses shod all around. Later, when I was working on the Plains, we never shod horses, except occasionally we had shoes put on one in order to make him more sure-footed.

It was customary to have a blacksmith do the shoeing. However, many of the large ranches either kept a blacksmith or had a cowboy who could shoe horses. The blacksmith's price for all-round shoeing was a dollar per horse. The blacksmith furnished and shaped extra shoes for fifteen cents each. These extra shoes could be fitted and nailed on by any cowboy. The average puncher took a great deal of pride in keeping his horse in good shape; consequently, he inspected, trimmed, and otherwise looked after his horse's feet with considerable care. Often when horses were being turned loose for long periods their shoes were removed, and, if still serviceable, were preserved for future use.

There were different types of shoes for various purposes. For riding horses an eight-ounce shoe was most common, while draft horses took a ten- or twelve-ounce shoe. A mule requires a differently shaped shoe than a horse, as his foot is narrower. Cowboys had their own terminology for the various types of shoes. A smooth shoe was called "a slipper,"

one with corked heel was "a shoe," while one with
both heel and toe corked was "a boot.'

Men who worked on the range a great deal became
very adept at obtaining information by noticing
tracks, especially those of shod horses and mules.
Many times a man would know by the tracks just
what horses made them and what their intentions
were at the time. Certain horses in a group have their
associates, or "chums," just the same way as people
do. If a person knows the tracks of two particular
"chums" in a group, he can make out something about
the movement of the herd by following these two
sets of tracks. If the horses were grazing, the tracks
will likely separate. If the horses were going somewhere in a walk, the tracks will be close together. If
they were being driven rapidly the tracks will probably come together, separate, and come together again
at intervals.

One morning in the late fall of 1878 while I was
still waiting on the Ranger vacancy, I was going along
the Llano River about daybreak in search of a turkey
roost. I soon located a roost, and was going up a path
along the river bank trying to get in range for killing
two or three turkeys with one shot when I heard a
noise in front of me. I looked down the path and
saw a big javelina sow and two pigs coming toward
me. I had seen javelinas before, but never at close
range. I understand that they are the only indigenous
species of hog family in America. A grown javelina
is about three feet long, and his body is thick up and
down, but thin and rangy horizontally. He has a long

head and snout, and the length of his head is about
a third of that of his body. A javelina's teeth are different from a hog's. His upper tusks are directed
downwards, and are very sharp; he uses them most
effectively in a fight. His bristles are much thicker,
longer, and coarser than a hog's. The bristles are
especially long on his throat, head, and nape of his
neck. The color of a javelina is grey with the ends
of the hair slightly frosted. The hair seems to be
more grey in the winter than summer. I don't know
whether the color actually changes with the seasons,
or whether the deadened hue of vegetation in winter
only makes it appear to change. I have seen two kinds
of javelinas, one with a solid color, and one with a
white band, or collar, behind its shoulders.

I understand that Indians, Mexicans, and some
white people eat the javelina. The meat is darker
and tougher than a hog's meat. The javelina has a
musk-bag located on his rump, and when he becomes
agitated he gives off a fatty substance with a most
offensive odor. I am told that people who kill the
javelina for food cut this bag off immediately after
killing him to prevent its contaminating the flesh. I
skinned a large boar one time and had a pair of chaps
made of the hide. I never did like the chaps; they
were too stiff and hard. I tried to wear them a short
time and gave them away.

Javelinas usually go in pairs, but I have seen them
in bunches with as many as a dozen in a group. They
are unlike hogs in that they never have but two pigs
at a time. They raise their young in caves, holes in

the ground, and hollow trees. They live on meat of such animals as they catch and vegetable matter, such as nuts, fruit and roots.

Javelinas are ferocious fighters, and will never run from a man. When I saw this old sow and two pigs coming down the path towards me, I did some quick thinking. I had only a shot-gun with me, and it was loaded with small shot. Suppose I should take a shot at the old sow and only wound her. That would mean that I would have to run for it, and a rangy javelina can run almost as fast as a horse. I decided not to take a chance with the shot-gun; and instead, I laid the gun down and climbed a tree. The old sow stopped, inspected my gun, looked up at me, grunted, smacked her jaws a few times, and passed on down the trail with the pigs behind her. I stayed in the tree until they were out of sight, and then came down and went after the turkeys. I killed two with one shot.

A few weeks later another puncher and I saw a javelina go in a cave near the top of the river bank. We left our horses and climbed up within ten feet of the mouth of the cave. Directly a big boar came to the entrance and started snapping his jaws at us and giving off that outlandish smell. We shot him with our Colt 45. Then another one came out, and we shot him. They kept coming until we killed a half dozen. When no more came we decided there were no more in the cave but we didn't go in to see. We considered we had made a pretty good hog-killing, anyway.

A short time before Christmas, 1878, while I was still riding the grub line a couple of men in Junction asked me to go turkey hunting with them. There were plenty of turkeys within a few miles of Junction, but they had been shot at, and were so wild you couldn't get within a mile of them. We put some camp equipment in a wagon and pulled out up the North Llano River about twenty-five miles from town and about thirteen miles above the Ranger camp. Just before sundown we found the signs of a big turkey roost along the river. We made our camp about a half mile down the river, cooked supper, and waited for the turkeys to come in. About sundown we heard them coming and going to roost. They were flapping their wings and clucking, and every once in awhile a limb would break. It was fully an hour from the time they started coming in until they all got quiet. There must have been thousands of them, for the trees were full for a quarter of a mile up the river.

Then we had to wait for the moon to come up so we could get a "bead." As a rule the turkeys on the same limb turn their heads in the same direction. I have seen as many as fifteen or twenty turkeys on one limb. When one is fortunate enough to get several heads in a line, he can kill several at one shot. Three were the most I ever killed at once, but I have frequently killed two.

When the moon got up a piece, all three of us maneuvered around for position. When we started banging, the turkeys started squawking, sputtering,

flying, and lunging in all directions; but not until we
had brought down twenty-four of them. Some of
them were so fat that they burst when they hit the
ground. We had to make two trips to carry the
twenty-four to camp, and carrying four big turkeys
at a time for a half mile was a big job. Then we
had to spend half the night dressing the turkeys.
The next morning we broiled twenty-four gizzards
for breakfast. When we started in, I thought that
making away with eight gizzards would be easy, but
we had gizzard for dinner. The second night, we got
thirty-two turkeys. We went back to town the next
day, taking enough Christmas turkeys for the entire
population of Junction.

A short time later I started from Junction to
Menardville (later called Menard). I was still riding the chuck line. It is about thirty-three miles
from Junction to Menardville, but was much farther
the way I went. I rode up the North Llano to the
Ranger camp where I stopped for dinner. In the
afternoon I travelled up Bear Creek to the head of
the Canyon. This route took me out of the brush onto
the open prairie. At the head of the Canyon was a
small spring of good water, surrounded by a little
plot of level ground some forty by sixty feet. The
plot was inclosed on three sides by a high rock bluff.
It was getting dark when we got there, and I thought
it would be a good place to camp. I did not want to
camp on the prairie, for Mescalero Apache Indians
were still raiding through that country, and they
could have seen my campfire for miles. I had scarce-

ly pulled my saddle off my horse, when I heard a
rattlesnake begin to sing (rattle). Then another on
the other side started. That seemed to be a signal for
a whole concert. It was soon evident that the Canyon
was full of snakes. There must have been a hundred
or more within fifty feet of me. Little snakes, big
snakes, and middle-sized snakes were all shaking
their tails at the same time, and the stench they
turned loose would have "made the devil sick at his
stomach." Neither my horse nor I had any inclina-
tion to stay at that snake pow-wow. It took me less
than half a minute to put my saddle on my horse and
mount him, and we "got a move on". My horse was
scared worse than I was, and that was saying a great
deal. He scarcely touched the ground, and we went
out of that Canyon like an old maid escaping from a
room full of mice. We spent an hour finding the
most unsnaky spot in the vicinity, and that was out on
the open prairie. We camped without a fire, and it
was a frosty night. A few years later the Rangers had
a skirmish with the Indians at the spring where the
rattlesnakes routed my horse and me. I am sure, however, if the rattlesnakes had been in session there at
the time, that neither the Indians nor the Rangers
would have been there.

In the spring of 1879 I went on a scouting expedition with Lieutenant L. B. Sieker. He was looking
for some Mexican cattle rustlers who had been operating rather extensively in the Devil's River country.
We went to Beaver Lake and then on to Dry Devil's

River. We saw lots of dry, rough country, but no rustlers.

When we returned, Captain Roberts told me that the vacancy I had been waiting for almost a year would materialize in about thirty days. As irony would have it, however, I found a letter waiting for me at the same time from my father telling me that my brother just younger than I was dangerously ill, and that I should hurry home at once. I saddled one of my horses, packed the other one, and left for home immediately. It took me eight days to make the trip of over three hundred miles. When I arrived I found brother convalescing. I could have gone back and probably have become a Ranger, but the year I had waited together with the fact that something might turn up to prevent my appointment caused me to decide to give up the idea of being a Ranger. Somehow I never regretted the decision either, for I afterwards found out that the man who got the vacancy was killed in a battle with some outlaws.

CHAPTER VI

COW-HUNTS AND NESTERS

I REMAINED at home from the fall of 1879 until the spring of 1880. In March I went to Jack County to look for a cow punchin' job, and got one from Hale, Dunn and Henson. They had only about 1,200 cattle, but they paid me thirty dollars a month, good pay for those days.

Cattle had drifted considerably from their ranges during the winter. The fencing of ranches or general round-ups had not yet come into vogue. The cattlemen of Clay, Montague, Jack, Wise, Palo Pinto and Parker Counties met at Jacksboro early in the spring of 1880 and organized a *cow-hunt*. This was not a general round-up, but strictly a cow-hunt on a large scale. There were about ten wagons with eight men, a boss, and a cook to each wagon. These outfits started on the south line of Palo Pinto and Parker Counties and began to work north. The wagons were strung out over a space of about fifty miles, and each wagon had a strip of about five miles to work. It was understood that no outfit was to get very far ahead of the others. Each wagon boss sent word to the neighboring wagons twice a week as to his progress, and in that way the wagons managed to keep fairly well in line. Every man had a list of brands belonging to the cattlemen participating in the hunt. The punchers rode through the range examining all cattle found. When they found animals bearing the brands they were looking for, they drove them to the herd which two of the boys were holding at the wagon.

I was with the wagon farthest east. Our oufit worked up the east line of Parker, Wise and Montague Counties. Our wagon and boss, whose name was Gibson, represented Stevens and Worsham in Clay County. We worked in pairs, and Henry Hensley was my partner. We all called him "Gawk". The name well described him, but he was a bully good fellow and a top hand.

When we got into the Cross Timbers, we found the log cabins of a good many nesters who had setled in the valleys. As a rule, these people had little and lived on the ragged edge. We found that many of the cows we were gathering were being milked by the nesters. One day we found a cow bearing Hensley's brand near a settler's place. The cow showed indications of suckling a calf. We drove the cow to the nester's cow-lot and turned her in, and a calf began to suck. A boy about ten years old came running out from the cabin and wanted to know what we were after. Hensley wanted to know how long they had been milking this cow. The boy said about four years. Hensley asked what they had done with her calves. The boy said he did not know exactly, but thought they had killed some for beef. There was an unbranded bull yearling in the lot. We took the cow, calf and bull yearling. As we drove them past the house, the woman with a half dozen brats holding on to her patched skirt came to the door and looked daggers at us. I felt a little bit reluctant about driving off these people's chief source of existence, but consoled myself by thinking that in a few days they would be milking somebody else's cow. We found some nesters who had milked cows so long (and had perhaps eaten the calves) that they protested vigorously about our driving the cows off.

Gawk and I played a risky and foolish prank during this hunt. Between Decatur and Paradise we saw the mail stage coming. Gawk suggested that I get on one side of the road and that he get on the other, and thus we would play stage robbers and hold up the driver. I was in for it. Just before we got to him we slipped our handkerchiefs over our faces and drew our Colts. We stopped and told him to "stick 'em up". He did, and looked mighty serious about it. I guess it was a good thing we didn't carry the joke any farther, as we might have done if we had had more time to plan it. We pulled down the handkerchiefs, and told the driver that we were really not stage robbers, but just a couple of punchers on a cow hunt. He seemed immensely pleased at that and laughed at our joke. That night while eating supper at the wagon, we told the boys about our escapade. Some of the boys were quite thrilled about it, but the boss didn't seem so thrilled. Then he told us how serious it was to hold up a United States mail.

He said it was mighty risky to monkey with Uncle
Sam's business. That put things in a different aspect.
I lay awake awhile that night thinking, and wondering if the driver would report us. I didn't think
he would, because he laughed as he drove off, but
then I couldn't help worrying just a little about it.
Before I went to sleep I resolved never to hold up
any more mail stages.

It took about thirty days to work from the south
line of Palo Pinto and Parker Counties to Red River.
When the hunt was over, all the outfits came together
and consolidated the herds. Then we cut out the cattle belonging to the various cowmen. Then the boys
representing the different cattlemen took their respective herds and started to their home ranges.

During the summer and early fall of 1880, I
branded, herded and wrangled for Hale, Dunn and
Henson. One day in October I rode out on the range
where my mount of horses was hobbled to catch a
fresh horse. He was wild, and I had to rope him.
Just as I threw the lariat the horse I was riding
stepped in a hole with both front feet and turned-a-
cat, heels over head. I hit the ground solid and passed
out for awhile. When I came to, the horse I had
been riding was standing nearby holding the other
horse. I had not known what I did with the rope, but
it had evidently gone true. I did not think I was
hurt until I started to get into the saddle. Then I
found my collar bone and right shoulder were brok-
en. I had to walk a mile back to camp.

The next morning, Mr. Hale took me to Jacksboro to a doctor to get my bones set. The doctor worked on me an hour, and thought he had everything fixed. We went back to the ranch and several days passed without any relief from the pain. Mr. Hale then proposed to take me to Denison in his two-horse hack. That ride was one long torture. I had a mattress to lie on, but found it less painful to sit up. It took two days to get to Denison. The doctor there found the bones all out of place again, and worked two long hours getting them set. He did a poor job of it, and my shoulder has bothered me ever since. I could never rope so well after this accident. I could still throw a short lariat all right, but I was not nearly so accurate on a long lariat.

I stayed at home until March, 1881, when I got a letter from Hale, Dunn and Henson, stating they wanted me to start working for them on April first. They inclosed a check for $75, saying they had decided to give me half pay while I was convalescing. That was a big surprise for me; getting pay for staying at home and doing nothing was almost too good to be true. I worked for them from April until July when they sold their cattle. Mr. Hale went to Fort Worth to become editor of *The Texas Livestock Journal*, published by George B. Loving.

CHAPTER VII

THE "22" RANCH

About the time Hale, Dunn and Henson sold their cattle, John Hensley from the Hensley Brother's Ranch in Crosby County came to Jacksboro. I was looking for a job, and he was needing a puncher; so we soon struck a bargain.

John and Charles Hensley, uncles of Gawk, had drifted their cattle from Jack County to the head of McDonald Creek in Crosby County in 1879. Their ranch was known as the "22" outfit. The headquarters consisted of a half dug-out about ten by twenty feet dug in the side of the creek bank. The walls were built up about three feet high with poles. The roof was made by placing poles close together and covering them with buffalo hides. There were not any windows at all. In the back side was a fireplace on which the cooking was done. In the winter time the boys slept on the floor, and in the summer they slept out of doors.

About two hundred yards east of Hensley's dugout were Will (W. B.) Slaughter's headquarters. Will was more pretentious than the Hensley's. He had a four-room "boxed" house. He had hauled the

72

lumber from Fort Worth in 1878. The Slaughter outfit used water from the same spring as the "22" outfit.

The Hensleys had about five thousand head of cattle and employed from four to six hands. I arrived with John in July and did general range duty until September. I had been working only a few days when the boss sent me to Singer's Store to mail a letter. This store and another owned by DeQuazy, a Frenchman, were located on the headwaters of Yellow House Creek about three miles above where Lubbock now stands.

Lured by the buffalo trade, George W. Singer had ventured out on the Plains with a wagon load of lumber and a wagon load of merchandise in 1879. He went up Yellow House to the last hole of living water, and there built a square "boxed" storehouse with his lumber, unpacked his goods, and started waiting for customers. They were slow in coming, for the hunters were leaving the range, and not many cowboys had as yet arrived. However, two military trails crossed at this waterhole, one from Fort Griffin to Fort Sumner, New Mexico, and the other from Fort Stockton to Fort Elliott. Few people traveled the Fort Stockton-Fort Elliott road, but quite a few cattle herds went out the McKenzie trail to Fort Sumner, and the cowboys contributed to Singer's business. With the country below filling up with cattle, the prospect bid fair for a brisk trade in the future—so much so that DeQuazy soon came in and put up a store within a hundred yards of Singer's.

Neither of them had any live stock except a freighting outfit each. They hauled their goods from Fort Griffin and Fort Worth.

DeQuazy didn't stay long. There was not enough business for two stores, and he could not compete with Singer. He might sell his goods cheaper, but he just didn't know how to get along with frontier people. Singer's house became known far and wide as Old Man Singer's Store.

"When the cowboys pushed up the Canyon with their cattle, he was there. When the round-ups drew to a close and jingling spurs struck music from the floor of his store, Old Man Singer was in his glory. Pack horses were hobbled out, bed rolls thrown upon the floor, and when night came the old man left the cowboys in charge and went home. Until far, far in the morning the good old game of poker held forth in earnest. When money was gone, a cowboy reached up and pulled down a box of stick candy or a plug of tobacco from a shelf, 'sweetened the pot', and the game went on. Another went broke, and another, and down came a pair of California pants to be bet against a couple of shirts. Singer appeared in the morning after the struggle was over. Never did a padlock fasten his door, and never was his confidence betrayed to the loss of a cent by these men who gambled in zest, but would have shot at a word."[1]

My boss gave me directions as to how to find Singer's store. I went south and southwest until I struck the Yellow House about the north line of Garza County. I was then on the north edge of the Curry Comb range of Young and Galbraith. Going up the Yellow House in the extreme southwest edge of Crosby County I came to the L A N C Ranch owned by W. R. Moore. Just south of Moore and

---

[1]Haley, J. E., *The XIT Ranch of Texas*, 50-51.

west of the Curry Combs was the range of Sam
Gholson, who had at that time about 2,500 cattle on
Spring Creek. Up the Yellow House just west of the
east line of Lubbock County was the ranch of the
Kidwell Brothers. Their brand was K I D. Several
miles above the Kidwell's dugout I came to Buffalo
Springs where a few years before the Causey boys
had their buffalo camp. Someone else was then occupying the old Causey dugout, but nobody was at
home. There were three or four hens clucking about
the camp, so I decided to get my dinner there. I
found two eggs and one can of tomatoes in the dugout, and I had eggs and tomatoes for dinner. Three
miles up the creek, I came to Z. T. Williams' sheep
ranch. There was a rock sheep corral and a "boxed"
house. A good spring of water high up on the cliff
made the location a desirable one. Ten miles farther
up I rounded a bend in the Canyon and saw Singer's
store, diminutive and forlorn, nestling on the southwest side of a lake which formed the headwaters of
the Yellow House. The lake covered several acres
and was fed by springs. When I rode up, a dozen or
more horses were tied to the hitching rack out in
front. In and around the store was a motley crowd
of cowboys, a few Mexicans, and a half dozen Apache
Indians. I mailed my letter, bought a drink of whiskey and some candy, stood around awhile, and started
back.

A short time after I made the trip to Singer's
Store, one of the boys went to Dockum's Ranch and
brought back news of Charley Dockum's being cap-

tured by the Indians. W. C. Dockum, Charley's father, had opened a supply store in a dugout on Dockum's Creek in the west part of Dickens County for buffalo hunters in 1877. When cattlemen began to bring in cattle and establish ranches, Dockum's business increased and he built a "boxed" house and moved out on top of the ground. Dockum was appointed postmaster, and for awhile Dockum's Ranch was the only postoffice northwest of Fort Griffin.

In the summer of 1881, Charley, then about fourteen, and another boy about twelve, were about three miles north of Dockum's looking for some horses. Some Indians saw the boys and gave them a chase. The other got away, but the Indians caught Charley. He expected to be murdered and scalped but instead, the Indians gave him a good whipping and turned him loose. Charley didn't lose any time getting home.

In September I was sent to "rep" (represent the outfit at outside round-ups) for the "22's" at the fall round-ups down the Double Mountain River. Although general round-ups had not yet been inaugurated, neighboring ranchmen coöperated as much as they possibly could in planning their work. I was the only one "reping" for the "22's" on the Double Mountain, and was attached to Will Slaughter's wagon.

The wagon had already worked through the O S range of Andy and Frank Long, which lay south of the Double Mountain River in the eastern part of Garza County, and was in the Two Circle Bar, OO range in the northeastern part of Scurry and north-

western part of Fisher Counties when I overtook it.
The Two Circle Bar ranch was owned by a Scotch-
man named Weirn. His foreman was Jim Lane, who
later, for some good reason, went under the name of
Jim Cook. When we got to the east side of the Two
Circle Bar range, in Stonewall County, we crossed
over to the north side of the river and started working back west. To the east of the place where we
crossed the river lay the H I T range of the Hitsons.
As we worked up the Double Mountain, we moved
from the Two Circle Bar range into the "80" range,
owned by Clay Mann. He was located north of the
river in the southeastern part of Kent County. Next
we came to Charley Dalton's range in the east central part of Garza County. Just northwest of Dalton
we worked through the range of Dan Kyle. Then we
entered the Curry Comb (〒) range of Young
and Galbraith in the northwest quarter of Garza
County. Turning north, we worked the range of
John (J. B.) Slaughter which lay between the Yellow House Fork of the Double Mountain and Mc-
Donald Creek. Just north of John's lay Will
Slaughter's range to the east of McDonald. We
ended the work on the "22" range just north of John
Slaughter's and west of McDonald. L. A. Wilson,
a son-in-law of John Hensley, owned the Paddle
brand, (ꝑ), and ranged with the Hensleys.

Late in the fall of 1881, after the round-ups
were over, Will Sanders and I were looking for some
"22" cattle to the southwest of the "22" range. We
had crossed the Yellow House and were traveling up

a little stream known as Harvey Creek which heads at the Cap Round southeast of where Slaton was later located. In a hackberry grove near the Caprock we found the bleaching skeleton of a man. His clothes had been ripped away and his flesh pecked and gnawed by buzzards and vermin. Near by were the remains of his saddle, pack saddle, and some broken arrows. Down the creek not far away were grazing four burros, as fat as could be. Every indication pointed to the conclusion that the man had been killed by the Indians two or three years before. We surmised that he had been with the buffalo hunters, and had started to Fort Griffin for a supply of provisions, and had gotten this far when the Indians found him.

In December, 1881, the "22's" established a winter camp on the Salt Fork of the Brazos about twelve miles south of the camp on the head of McDonald Creek. Van Sanders was boss, and John Garrison, Will Sanders and myself made up the winter crew. We located the camp on a little bluff on the north side of the river. It was a dugout about the same size as the one on McDonald. It took us several days to make the excavation, and we didn't like the digging much. We did not build up the walls any with poles, because poles were scarce, and it was to be a temporary camp, anyway. The pole roof was about five feet above the floor, and we had to stoop when we walked around. We first thought we would not need a door, but the first cold weather came from the east and caused us to change our minds. We hustled around

and made a door out of a dried beef hide. The fireplace was in the back side.

We transported our camp equipment from Mc-
Donald Camp on our horses, but that was not much
of a job. We had two Dutch ovens—one for meat
and one for bread—a frying pan, a coffee pot, a
butcher knife, three or four sacks of flour and a few
pounds of salt and coffee. Our beds consisted of a
number of wolf hides with a few blankets for cover.
The beds were made down on the dirt floor around
the walls of the dugout. The hides were from wolves
we had killed on the range. They were full of fleas
when first killed, but fleas soon leave a dead hide.
We brought in a number of buffalo skulls to sit on.
We had no table of any kind. Our camp light was
a tin can filled with tallow (rendered up from
beeves) with cotton rags torn in strips and plaited
for wicks.

After we got our camp made we had a few days
of idle time, and we decided to get in our winter's
supply of wood. We had no wagon, so we got on our
horses and started out to look for dead mesquite
limbs and roots. This kind of wood was plentiful in
the arroyos leading into the river. We would rope
limbs and break them off with the rope tied to the
saddle horn. Then we would make up a bundle of
wood and drag it to camp. We liked this kind of
work a lot better than we did the digging. In a few
days we dragged up enough wood to last all winter.

There were lots of wild hogs in the country. Wher-
ever we found shinery (sandy land covered with

scrub oak) we found wild hogs. It was said that a
man had started a hog ranch in the shinery in Dickens
County in 1877; and a year or two later after he was
killed by the Indians his hogs went wild. I never
knew for sure whether this was the way hogs came
to be in the region or not, but when I arrived in July,
1881, there were hogs and lots of them. You could
not ride over a mile or two in the shinery without
jumping some. They didn't hear a horse coming until
you were right on them; then they would charge
away, snorting and grunting all at once and making
a noise like a person shifting gears in an old worn-
out car. They never failed to scare your horse, and
he could come well-nigh setting you on your head.

The hogs were of all colors—white, black, yellow,
spotted, big spots, little spots and speckled. There
were two things they all had in common, however—
long snouts and long legs. They were probably of
rather primitive stock to start with, and nature had
helped to lengthen snouts and legs since they had
gone wild. Only those survived which had the longest snouts to fight and dig with and the longest legs
to run with. It was these which lived to propagate
the species. They were usually lean and lanky, but
when the acorn crop was good in the shinery they
put on a little fat. I seldom ever found one, however, that weighed over one hundred and fifty
pounds.

Wild hogs, as a rule, scattered out when looking
for food, but when attacked, all within hearing distance would bunch up. They would get the pigs in

the center, and the old ones would keep to the outside of the circle with their heads turned out. The
old boars had long tusks, and could deal dreadful
havoc in a fight. A panther or lobo could make an
easy killing of a pig or half-grown shoat, but shied
off from an old boar. If the hogs had a chance to
gang up after the alarm was given, they were safe.

After we got the wood in, Van Sanders and John
Garrison left camp for a few days on a cow hunt.
Before he left, Van told Will and me to go up in the
shinery, kill some hogs, and render out some lard.
We shot two fairly fat hogs about a mile and a half
from camp, dragged them to camp by the saddle
horn and skinned them.

We had no kettles for scalding hogs in the conventional way, but we had three fairly good sub-
stitutes. One method was to dig a hole in the ground,
fill it with water, and heat the water by dropping hot
stones in it. Water can be made to boil in a short time
after the stones are heated. As the stones are dropped
in the water, the heat passes from the stones to the
water with great rapidity. Indians used this method
of heating for cooking. We could get a good scald in
this way. It was a good method to use when one
wanted to cure the meat, as it preserved the hide.

When we wanted fresh meat and did not want to
take time to heat stones, we skinned the hogs. There
were two ways of skinning. If there was a tree nearby large enough to hold a hog, we strung him up
by the hind legs, and took the skin off in strips about
two or three inches wide. If there were no trees con-

venient, we skinned the hog on the ground. We
turned him on his back, began in the middle of his
belly, and skinned the hide down both sides, like
one would do a buffalo or a beef.

We got about twenty pounds of lard from our two
hogs besides the meat. We rendered the lard, a little
at a time, in the Dutch ovens. When we finished, we
thought we had done a big day's work. The next
day we rode the south line of our range to see if any
cattle had crossed recently. When we got back late
in the afternoon, we found that something had entered our camp and destroyed our supply of meat and
lard. We started an investigation and found hog
tracks all over the place. We followed them away
from the camp towards the shinery and overtook a
rangy sow and a bunch of shoats. We decided they
were the culprits, pulled our 45's, and had another
hog-killing. We spent the rest of the evening skinning, and the next day rendering.

During the winter we rode the south line of our
range. To the west the line extended to the Caprock
about fifteen miles distant. It crossed a ridge between
the Salt Fork and Yellow House Creek. A short time
after the hog-killing, Will Sanders and I were riding
across this ridge one day and found the carcass of a
cow which had been killed but a few hours. We got
off our horses and started to look for evidence which
would indicate how she was killed. We found she
had been shot with arrows. One arrow was still sticking in the under side. The Indians had taken most of
the meat, and had stripped and taken the intestines.

Indians considered the intestines the best part of a
cow or buffalo. They were like lobos and eagles in
that respect. They would kill a cow; and before she
was through kicking, they would rip out the intestines and start eating them raw. They claimed the
juices in the intestines were good for them. Will and
I figured that the Indians might still be lurking
somewhere about, and they could see a long way on
that ridge, so we didn't lose any time in getting away
from there. We called the place Indian Ridge, and
it still goes by that name today.

CHAPTER VIII

A FRONTIER BALL

THE winter of 1881-1882 was a gay one for the cowboys of Crosby, Floyd, Motley, Dickens, Kent, Garza, Lynn and Lubbock Counties. We had two dances, one at Will Slaughter's in January, and one at Dockum's in March. The one at Dockum's was scheduled to take place first, but had to be postponed about three months.

We were all excited about the dances, and had been for weeks. Ever since the fall round-ups were over, practically all of our talk had been about the forthcoming dances. We started getting ready for Slaughter's dance a week before it began. I had brought three white shirts from home. They had been white before I left home, but hanging around in a dugout for six months had changed their color. Will Sanders, John Garrison and I conceived the idea of washing these shirts and "putting on some dog" at the dance. We didn't have any place to wash them but the creek, and the water there was of a reddish, muddy hue. We washed them all right, but when we got through the shirts were a streaked pink color.

The next day Will Sanders came by L. A. Wilson's dugout over on Pole Canyon and found a smoothing iron and about four pounds of starch. Mrs. Wilson had left these articles at the dugout the previous fall when she and her husband returned to Jacksboro. (Wilson ranged with the Hensleys, and our outfit looked after his cattle during the winter). It had not occurred to us that we ought to starch or iron our shirts, but when Will saw that starch and smoothing iron, the idea struck him, and he came wagging them into camp, looking a little sheepish. The idea went over big with John and me, and we got busy at once. We filled one of the Dutch ovens two-thirds full of water and put in about two and one-half pounds of starch. We got it boiling and then baptized the shirts. Then we hung them out on bushes to dry. We didn't wring them any, because we didn't want to lose any of our precious starch. When they got dry, they seemed to be starched a-plenty. They were hard as boards and would stand alone. We were puzzled, then, as to how to get them ironed. One of the boys remembered seeing his mother sprinkle clothes before ironing; then we all remembered having seen that done at home. We sprinkled the shirts and they would still stand alone. We tried to put them on and failed at that. John suggested, maybe, we had used too much starch. So we made up another batch, this time putting in about half as much starch. When it got to boiling, we stuck the shirts in. They collapsed slowly like a hard lump of sugar melting at the bottom. When

they dried, they would still stand alone. We didn't
realize that all the starch of the first dipping was still
in the shirts. We took the shirts to the creek and let
them soak while we got some chuck. We had been
so busy that we had let half the afternoon slip by
without realizing it was time to eat. After chuck, we
got ready to iron, but when we brought our shirts
out they were as limber as a rawhide string that had
been left in the water overnight. Will suggested that
we give them another starching, but we found we had
used all the starch. Then we proceeded with the ironing. The iron had rust on it, and when we finished,
our shirts were a yellowish pink with brown spots
from the iron all over them. We looked them over
and decided it was a failure. We had spent the better
part of two days and all Mrs. Wilson's starch and
made a bad job of it. I suppose that if the starch and
shirts had held out we would have stayed at it several days. As it was, we had to wear old cow-punchin'
togs to the dance. We washed them out in the creek,
but didn't attempt the ironing business on them.

The morning before the dance was to start we
spent trying to shave. I had brought an old razor
with me, but none of us had tried to use it since I
arrived six months before. Our beards were full of
grit and none of us were very good at sharpening a
razor. We used the stirrup leather of a saddle for a
strop. We would pull at our whiskers awhile and
strop awhile. We didn't have a looking glass, so we
had to shave each other. Will and I got our beards
off after a fashion, but when John saw how much

blood we were bringing, he decided he would go to the dance with his beard intact.

We started at noon because it was twelve miles, and we wanted to arrive early. Others were already arriving when we got there. The women were coming in buckboards and hacks, and the men on horseback. We hobbled our horses out, and got ready for supper.

Will Slaughter had gotten ready for us in big style. He had barbecued a beef, had boiled a bunch of hams (of wild hogs), had roasted several turkeys, had several quarters of venison ready to cut into steaks, and antelope meat ready to be made into stew with "sinkers" (dumplings). Mrs. Slaughter had made several gallons of jelly and preserves from wild plums during the previous summer. She had cooked a tub full of doughnuts, stacks of fried apple pies, and some cakes—the first I had seen since I left home. The coffee pot was kept steaming until we left three days later.

There were nine women present, Mrs. Will Slaughter, Mrs. Sam Gholson and her two daughters from the extreme southeast corner of Lubbock County, Mrs. Coon Cooper from Garza County, two daughters of Joe Browning from Dickens County (one of them later married Jim McCommis), Miss Scarborough from Snyder, and Miss Rodie De Graffenried from Dickens County. There were so many cowboys they all couldn't get in the house at the same time; there were thirty or more. About dark George Edwards got out his old fiddle and

started tuning up.   He thumped, twisted, listened,
strummed, and sawed for a half hour. I couldn't
see that he was making much headway, but he finally
got it fixed to suit him and drew the bow vigorously
across the strings a few times by way of warming up.
Then Bill Petty, a six-footer with a pair of leather
lungs from the Spur range on Red Mud, bellowed,
"Get yer partners fer the first dance."

Most of the boys were kinda shy at first. They
had not been around women for so long that they
were a little afraid of them. Enough of the more
brazen ones got up sufficient courage to ask partners
for the first dance. Two rooms had been cleared for
dancing. They were so small that only one set could
dance in each room at a time. The fiddler sat in the
door between the two rooms.

When four couples had gotten out on the floor,
George Edwards struck up a tune and started keeping time energetically with his bootheel. Bill roared:

> "Two little sisters form a ring,
>   Don't forget to break and swing,
>   Partner with your right hand,
>   Corner with your left,
>   Partner with your right,
>   Right and wrong all night long,
>   Meet your partner and promenade home.
>
> "Three little sisters form a ring,
>   Don't forget to break and swing," etc.

George rested a moment and struck up another
tune. Bill shouted to the gents to get partners for

the next dance. The boys were not so shy this time.
Bill began:

> "Hark ye partners,
> Rights the same,
> Balance you all,
> First lady to the right;
> Swing the man who stole the sheep,
> Now the one that hauled it home,
> Now the one that ate the meat,
> Now the one that gnawed the bones.
>
> "First gent, swing yer opposite partner,
> Then yer turtle dove.
> Again yer opposite partner,
> And now yer own true love.
> First couple to the right,
> Cage the bird, three hands round.
> Birdie hop out and crane hop in,
> Three hands around, and go it again.
>
> "All men left; back to the partner,
> And grand right and left;
> Come to yer partner once and a half,
> Yeller hammer right and jaybird left,
> Meet yer partner and all chaw hay,
> You know where and I don't care,
> Seat yer partner in the old arm chair."

Three nights and two days—quadrilles, waltzes,
schottisches, and polkas. I wondered how the women
stood it. With the men it was different. There were
three times as many of them as women; consequently
they got to rest about two-thirds of the time. When

one of the boys got tired and sleepy, he could go out
to the half dugout used for a bunk house and get a
nap, but the women were not given much chance to
rest. However, they danced with minimum exertion. The men swung them so lustily that little effort
was necessary on their part. Before daybreak of the
third morning, however, their feet got tired and
sore.

A considerable amount of whiskey was in evidence,
among the men especially. None got drunk, but some
of them stayed pretty well keyed up.

On the morning following the third night of dancing we caught our horses and started back to camp,
a tired bunch. When we got there it was not to bed
and to sleep, but to work until dark. We had to ride
the line and make up for the three days we were
away. It was long after dark when we hit our wolf
hides. We were a week getting over the effects of the
dance, and I expect the women were longer than
that. Before long, however, we were getting excited
about the Dockum dance.

During the previous fall (1881), Mr. Dockum
hauled lumber from Fort Worth and started building his storehouse, twenty by thirty feet. We pre-
vailed on him to give us a Christmas tree and a
dance. He agreed to do so, provided we would guarantee to buy all his Christmas goods, and not leave
any on his hands unsold. Van and Will Sanders, Bill
and Tom Petty, Dick Crutchfield, John Garrison,
Jack Alley, several others and I made the guarantee. News of the dance spread counties around. When

Christmas came, neither all the lumber for the house nor the Christmas goods had arrived on account of bad weather delaying the freighters. About the first week in March, Dockum sent us word that the lumber and goods had arrived. Several of us who had guaranteed to take the Christmas wares got together and set a date for the Christmas tree. We put it two weeks off so the news would have time to get around. The day before the occasion, several of us went to the brakes over by the Caprock and brought in a big cedar for the Christmas tree. We put it up in the store and spent next day decorating it.

About the same crowd came to it that afternoon that had been at Slaughter's dance. The tree was as big a success as if it had taken place on scheduled time. Everyone was in a festive mood. I suppose this was the first community Christmas tree ever held west of Fort Griffin. The next year the Matadors had a delayed tree. It also took place in March, because the things that had been ordered for it were nearly three months late getting in.

After the Christmas tree exercises were over, we started to dance. George Edwards did the fiddling again and Bill Petty the calling. This dance was a one-night affair, and nobody lost any time. While the boys were waiting turns in the sets, they hustled the coffee pot and smoked cigarettes, occasionally taking a Christmas "nip" from a bottle of Four Roses.

A few days before the dance John Garrison burned a large hole in one of his boots while trying to dry it over the camp fire. John was in a bad frame of mind while we were making preparations. I saw he was dying with envy, so I had him try on my boots. They fitted him to a gnat's heel. I told him we would take it turn about; I would dance a set while he stayed outside the house, then I would go outside and let him wear my boots while he danced a set. We managed the thing so that no one suspected the exchange of footgear. That was one dance that my boots took part in nearly every set.

The dance broke up at sun-up, and we caught our horses and headed for our home ranges.

CHAPTER IX

"REPING" FOR THE "22" OUTFIT

WINTER work with the "22" outfit was strenuous, but not so much so as it had been with Mr. X's outfit in Clay County. We got up before daylight, made a fire in the fireplace, and three of us cooked breakfast while the other wrangled the horses. One of us made sourdough biscuits, another cooked the meat and made gravy, and the third made coffee and hustled the fire. While we were waiting for the bread to cook, we sat around on our heels and smoked cigarettes. Unless the horses had gotten too far away, the one on wrangle usually got in by the time the biscuits were done. We used our pocket knives for eating; we would take a biscuit, put a piece of meat on it, and hold it in our hands while we ate it. When we wanted gravy, we sopped in the skillet. We had some tin plates, but didn't use them in order to save dish washing. We had tin cups for coffee; and the cups and skillet were the only things we had to wash.

We had our horses saddled and were ready to start by daylight. Our horses were pretty well broke, but occasionally one would cut loose and buck awhile when we mounted on a cold morning. We rode the south line of our range each day, two of us going east and two going west. If we found fresh tracks crossing the trail, we took after them until we overtook the cattle and drove them back. We might find them within one mile or maybe ten. When we got that bunch back, we went on up the line trail looking for others. Some days we would get back to camp by the middle of the afternoon, and other days it would be after dark.

We seldom ever had anything to eat from the time we left until we got back. We were always as hungry as wolves when we got in. As soon as we could, we cooked some chuck. It consisted of biscuits, meat, gravy and coffee. The Hensleys brought our provisions from Jacksboro twice a year. About the only articles they ever furnished were flour, salt and coffee. We had to hustle our own meat, and did without sweetstuffs. We got pretty tired of just having biscuits, meat and gravy. One day one of the boys was at Dockum's and decided to buy some rice, on his own hook. None of us knew anything about cooking rice. We put a half gallon in a Dutch oven and started to boil it. It started swelling up and filled the oven. We put part of it in the other oven, and pretty soon had both ovens full. We put some in a small bucket and still there was not enough room. Then we piled some out on the ground. We had to eat all the rice in our bread oven before we could cook any more biscuits. We had rice for three days and were pretty well caught up on that cereal by the time we finished the batch.

In spite of our efforts, cattle drifted badly during the winter of 1881-1882. When spring came, a good many of the "22" cattle had gotten away from us and had drifted far to the south. In April, 1882, I was sent along with John Slaughter's wagon to work the C. C. Slaughter range which, at that time, began a few miles west of Colorado City and reached to the head of the Colorado River. "Lum" (C. C.) Slaughter had started out in Palo Pinto County during the early 50's. He had ridden after cattle bareback when he was too poor to own a saddle; he had freighted with an ox team from Jefferson; and he had trailed cattle from the Rio Grande to Kansas. In 1879 he realized that the day of free grass was over in Palo Pinto County, and moved his herds to Howard, Martin, Dawson and Borden Counties. He purchased some land there and leased a lot more—nearly a million acres in all. Gus (C. A.) O'Keefe was his manager.

O'Keefe knew how to manage men, and he had a good bunch to manage. To see him giving directions was inspiring. I think he was the first man I ever saw that stirred my ambition. He made me want to be a ranch manager and handle a crowd of punchers. Slaughter's outfit had ridden a close line on the south side of the range during the winter, and had kept the cattle of all brands to the north, as well as their own, from drifting south of the Texas and Pacific Railroad.

The round-up began on the head of Colorado

River and worked down the river. There were about
twelve wagons along with ten to twelve hands to
the wagon. O'Keefe would designate a place for
a round-up and send the various outfits in different
directions from the river to gather the cattle and
concentrate them at the round-up grounds.

One day after a heavy rain our outfit was laying
up, and John Gardner, John Bell, another puncher,
and I had been doing some exploring on our own
hook. We were returning to the wagon when we
jumped a panther. We took after him, and John
Gardner and I shot at him a few times. After a
half mile or so the panther bayed behind a bush.
Someone suggested that we rope the cat and take him
to camp alive. The plan sounded interesting, but I
don't think any one was particularly caring about
being the first one to lay his rope on the panther. We
flipped a coin to determine the order of roping. John
Gardner made the first run and put his lariat over
the cat's neck, but the panther flipped the loop off
with his paw. I made the second run and missed him
on purpose. John Bell made a try and the cat again
flipped the rope off. The fourth man didn't take
part. Gardner came next and missed. Again it was my
turn. I decided to try to put my rope on the crea-
ture this time, let happen what might. I ran within
fifteen feet of the cat and threw my loop. Then I
felt the rope grow taut. There I was with one end of
my rope around the saddle horn and the other end
around a live panther. My horse was going at full
speed, and the other boys said the panther was jerked

through the air for fifteen feet when my horse took up the slack. I drug the panther for a couple of hundred yards, and then stopped to see how he was coming. He was so groggy he was hardly able to stand. One of the shots we had taken at him had nipped off two or three toes on one foot. I supposed that was the reason he made the stand behind the bush. One of the boys threw another lariat on him and we held him between our horses so he couldn't do anything. We then took the horn strings off our saddles and tied his jaws and feet. We had to blindfold a horse before we could get him up to the panther. Then we put the panther across the saddle and tied him hard and fast. When we got to camp and unloaded the cat, the cook mounted the wagon and said, "Men, if you don't kill that varmint, I am quitting this outfit here and now!"

We killed the panther.

When the Lum Slaughter round-ups were over, we brought the "22" strays back with the John Slaughter strays. When we got to John Slaughter's place, his men helped cut the "22" strays and start them back to our range. Then I drifted them the rest of the way by myself. It was the last week in July when I arrived.

In the fall of 1882 the Hensley Brothers sent me to Bill McDonald's ranch at Big Salt Lake in New Mexico to purchase some bulls. They had heard that McDonald had some good ones to sell. It was one hundred and twenty miles out to Big Salt Lake. I got an early start and reached Williams sheep ranch by late noon. Mr. Williams was at home, so I stopped and ate dinner with him. I found he had come there in 1877 and acquired three sections of land. There was already a sheep corral at the spring before he located there. It had been built a year or two before by some "floater" passing through. In the summer of 1880, Williams had to go away from the ranch for several days. It was late at night when he returned. He noticed that the herder was missing, and that the sheep were not in the corral. Early next morning he started out to look for the herder and found him dead about a mile and a half from the house.

Some distance farther, Williams found the sheep. The herder's dog was still with them. The dog had kept the sheep together and guarded them for two days and nights. Williams buried the herder near the house. Afterwards a treasure legend got started in regard to the herder, his strange death, and burial, and people have been going to the old Williams ranch and digging for buried treasure ever since.

I spent that night at Singer's store. Next morning I purchased a supply of sardines, salmon, cheese, and crackers, and headed west. About three miles beyond Singer's store I noticed a man's footprints in the trail. The tracks were going the same way I was. I trailed those footprints all day. Late in the afternoon I reached Yellow House, a peculiar formation resembling a house from a distance; Yellow House Canyon took its name from this formation. At Yellow House the trail forked, one fork leading north-

west and the other, north. The tracks went north and
so did I. About two miles up this fork I met the man
coming back whose tracks I had been following all
day. He hailed me and asked where I was headed
for. I told him McDonald's ranch, and he said he
was going there too, but that we were on the wrong
road. The sun was almost down when we got back
to Yellow House. I proposed that we camp for the
night and he agreed.

I unsaddled my horse and staked him close to
my saddle. I noticed the stranger had only a water
bottle and a slicker. I asked him to eat with me, and
he did not need any urging, for he had not eaten anything since the evening before. When we bedded
down I put my head on my saddle and turned my
face toward the stranger. Soon I got to thinking,
"Suppose this fellow is an outlaw and tries to take
my horse and leave me afoot."

The more I thought the more convinced I was that
he was a bad man. I lay all night watching him. I
had my .45 in my hand, and if he had made a move
toward me or my horse, I would have shot him. But
he did not so much as turn over all night. Next
morning we ate what was left of my cheese and
crackers and started on. We stayed together for
awhile, but did not have much to say to each other.
I was thinking that he had escaped from some penitentiary, and he probably thought I was some horse
rustler or outlaw. After an hour or two I rode on
ahead, and got to McDonald's camp about 3 o'clock.
About sun-down the stranger came in. After supper

he and I got to talking. I learned that he had bossed a sheep herd from New Mexico to Colorado City to be sheared, and was on his way back to New Mexico after another herd. At that time the sheepmen of New Mexico were driving thousands of sheep to Colorado City and Big Spring to be sheared. In this way the sheep transported their own wool to the railroad shipping points as well as getting six months of free grazing while going and coming. Then the sheep would be slowly drifted back to their ranges in New Mexico by the herders.

Big Salt Lake was a treacherous place for sheep. As I approached that afternoon, I could see white spots all over the lake. I could not figure out what they were for awhile, but when I got to the edge, I saw they were the bodies of sheep sticking out of the water. The water was strong alkali, and the lake was boggy. Sheep were always bogging and drowning.

There were some fresh water springs on the north end of the lake where McDonald's camp was located. Doak Good moved his cattle to this lake the following winter, and a year or two later Jim Newman brought in his cattle. A short time after Newman arrived, he and Good got crossways, and finally had a shooting scrape at a round-up. Later, Good moved his cattle farther on, and Newman sold to the D Z outfit owned by Curtis and Lazarus.

I looked at McDonald's bulls, but did not buy any. The second morning after my arrival I started back. When I reached Silver Lake I saw five or six buffaloes at a distance. As the wind and some small sand

hills were in my favor, I decided to take a shot at
them. I dismounted and dropped the long bridle
reins. Cowboys always used long reins, and did not
tie the ends together. When a horse fell, or when a
rider was thrown from a horse, the reins would fall
to the ground, and the horse would step on the reins
and the rider would have a chance to catch the horse.

When I thought I was near enough to the buffaloes
I fired. They started in my direction on a run. I stood
up and began firing for the purpose of scaring them.
They ran past me and within fifty yards of my horse.
This scared him, and he started down the road. The
long reins prevented his making much speed, but he
had unusual intelligence; he held his head on one
side so he would not step on the reins. I followed
him about three miles and was not making much
headway in overtaking him. Then I remembered that
the trail where we were made a big bend; so I took
a short cut and managed to head him off.

I was so mad when I mounted that I took my six-
shooter and jabbed him on the head between the
ears. About the second jab, he fell as if he had been
"creased." He fell on my leg, and got up before I
did, and started down the road again. This time I
had to overtake him with a lame leg. It was a pretty
good lesson to me. It had not occurred to me that
most all horses are afraid of buffaloes. That night I
camped at Yellow House, the second night at Singer's store, and the third night I was back at the
"22" camp.

During the summer of 1882 the outfit moved back

to the camp at the head of McDonald. When the
fall work was over we went back to the camp on
Salt Fork on the south line of our range. Steve Mar-
timer, the man who had run into our trail camp in
Keechi Valley in 1873 when the Indians killed
Walker and his son, worked with us that winter.

Polecats were bad around the camp. They would
come into the dugout at night when we were asleep.
When we would hear the polecats coming, we would
cover our heads. They would walk over us, our beds,
and everything else in sight. They seemed to like
scraps of fried meat or anything that had grease on it.
We could not shoot them in camp for we would have
had to leave ourselves then.

One night while we were all asleep a cat bit Steve
between the eyes. Steve let out a yell that could
have been heard a mile away. We had to pull the
cat loose. It was a little striped cat, the kind that is
said to cause hydrophobia. Steve began to cry and
said he would go mad. All of us were afraid he would
start having fits. We kept a poultice of soda on the
wound for several days, and Steve began to calm
down. I told him he was scared worse than when the
Indians were after him in Keechi Valley. He said the
Indians gave him a chance to run and the polecats
didn't. He soon went back to Jacksboro, saying he
would not live in a country where the polecats ran
over him at night in droves.

We tried luring them away from the dugout by
putting fresh meat for them out in front, but that
didn't work. Then we got some dogs and tied them

in front of the door, but the cats got into the dugout, anyway. Finally we made it our business to hunt polecats about sundown; that is about the time they leave their dens. We killed a great number, and by spring had them about killed out around the camp.

Coyotes were numerous in our vicinity that winter. The sandy bed of the river was a quarter of a mile wide in front of our camp. The water sunk below the surface except after a heavy rain. We often saw coyotes playing up and down the river bed. After we got our dogs, they kept the coyotes chased off for awhile, but finally got to where they would play with them. The coyotes were smart. They would romp with the dogs until the dogs started toward the camp, and then they would stop. They consistently stayed out of the range of our Winchester rifles.

In March, 1883, Will Slaughter offered me thirty-five dollars a month to work for him. That was top wages in those days. Mr. Slaughter told me that I was an extra good hand and knew the game, and if I was offered more money than he was giving me, to accept without consulting him. The Hensley Brothers never acquired any land, and in 1885 sold the "22" cattle to Harrell, Franklin and Henson. These men ran the outfit for a short time and then sold the cattle off. Their range was being acquired and fenced by the Spurs.

I had worked for Slaughter only one month when Mr. German B. Stout of Kentucky offered me fifty dollars a month. Mr. Stout was a fine man, but a tenderfoot. He had located five hundred cattle on Yel-

low House Creek in Garza County, just east of the
Curry Combs, and his brand was "202".

As soon as I started working for Mr. Stout, I was
sent to represent the "202's" at the round-ups on the
Curry Comb range. A few days later we were holding a round-up about six miles north of the present
town of Post. A herd of buffaloes stampeded somewhere to the west of us and came thundering down
from the Plains, headed straight for our round-up.
Everything was in confusion. The cattle stampeded,
and all sixty of the cowboys quit the cattle and took
after the buffaloes. The boys who had pistols started
shooting; the others took their lariats and tried roping. I lost out early when my horse stepped in a hole
and fell just as I was coming alongside a big bull.
The others chased the herd several miles. When they
came straggling back, practically every one had a
big yarn to tell about how he had shot or roped a
buffalo. An actual count, however, disclosed that only
twelve buffaloes had been killed. We had buffalo
meat for several days.

A few days after this, Comanche Indians raided
the Llano (Curry Comb) Ranch and drove off
twenty horses. Mr. Galbraith, the manager, tracked
the Indians to Fort Sill and found the horses in a
Comanche camp. Galbraith claimed the horses. The
Indians were quite willing to turn the horses over
to him, but said that Galbraith would have to pay ten
dollars a head to get them out of the Indian country.
Galbraith argued with them, but to no avail. He
knew better than to start without satisfying the In-

dians; so he paid them two hundred dollars, and the Indians helped him get the horses across Red River.

CHAPTER X

THE LLANO RANCH

WHILE I was staying at the winter camp on the Salt Fork and riding the "22's" south line during the winters of 1881-1882 and 1882-1883, I occasionally met Mr. Ben Galbraith, manager of the Llano Cattle Company. Our south line was the Llano's north line. Our cattle would sometimes become mixed during a bad spell of weather, and the Llano outfit would help us separate them. In this way I got to know Mr. Galbraith quite well, and our friendship eventually led to my promotion.

In 1875 Colonel W. C. Young of Fort Worth had purchased three hundred stock cattle and put Ben Galbraith, a young Irishman from Illinois, in charge. They kept the cattle in Tarrant County for a year, then moved them to Shackelford County. At the time of the move, Young made Galbraith an equal partner and they started the Y G brand. Three years later (1879) they moved the herd to Garza County, and made a dugout camp on Yellow House Creek about ten miles north of where Post was later located. The next year they organized the Llano Cattle Com-

106

pany with a capital of $400,000. W. C. Young was
president and Ben Galbraith manager. Sam S. Gholson turned in 2,500 cattle and received $50,000 in
stock. E. T. Ambler of Fort Worth and T. J. Lycon
of Dallas were heavy stockholders. S. A. Johnson,
one of the cowboys, and Ed Ryan, red-headed bookkeeper on the ranch, had a few shares each. There
were other stockholders whose names I have forgotten. Jasper Hays surveyed the lands, thumping along
on his wooden leg. Aside from the three hundred
original cattle, the Llanos never bought any cattle
except the 2,500 head Gholson put in. By 1883 the
herd numbered between 8,000 and 10,000. At the
time of its organization the Llano Company dropped
the Y. G. brand and started the Curry Comb,   .
The Company also began buying and leasing land
and eventually acquired a tract twelve by sixteen
miles.

The Llano range was watered by natural water-
courses. Yellow House Creek ran through the northeast corner. Several creeks headed at the foot of the
Caprock and ran into Yellow House. These creeks
had springs at their sources.

About the last of June, 1883, Mr. Galbraith came
to me and said he was going to leave the ranch for
at least a year. His health was failing, and he was
having trouble. In fact, if the threats meant anything,
his life was in danger. He said he was going to Fort
Worth in a few days and intended recommending me
to the officials of the company as his successor. I
could hardly believe my ears—here was my one am-

bition about to be realized. In a few days a letter came from Colonel Young directing me to take charge of the ranch on August 1. Mr. Galbraith never returned; he went to his old home in Illinois and died shortly. His interest in the Llano Cattle Company was inherited by his brother, Dave.

Sam Gholson had been after me for sometime to go with him on a hunt for some horses that had been running with mustangs since 1880. In June of 1880 a friend of Gholson's from Coleman County had been taking sixty cow ponies to New Mexico to sell. About where Levelland is now located, the horses had stampeded and got mixed with mustangs. The driver had been unable to round them up, and the horses had been running wild ever since. I had told Gholson that I thought it would be a wild-goose chase, but after I got Colonel Young's letter appointing me as manager of the Llano Ranch, I decided to take the month of July off and go with Gholson.

We took two horses each, some chuck and a pair of fieldglasses, and spent two days riding over the western part of Lubbock County and the eastern part of Hockley County. Grass was good and the lakes were full of water. We saw lots of mustangs. They were in bands numbering from twenty to fifty, and each band was led by a stallion. When we ran short of chuck we headed for Estacado. We were looking pretty seedy when we got to Charles Holmes' store, and most every man and boy in the village came in to look us over. Gholson described the horses we were looking for and asked if anyone had seen such a bunch. Lint Hunt said he had watched a bunch of mustangs at a lake ten miles west of Estacado a few days before, and he thought some of them were branded.

We went out to the lake he told us about and camped. The next morning we scouted around several hours and found the herd. With the aid of the fieldglasses we discovered that some of the horses were branded. Gholson was for capturing them, and I told him I had as soon chase this bunch as any other on the Plains.

We hobbled our extra horses near the lake and started the long, continuous run which was eventually to tire the mustangs out. I took the first shift while Gholson went to our camp by the lake and ate supper. The horses ran about five miles in one direction, but finally turned back to our camp. After this first run they never went over three miles from our camp; this was their range. I kept close enough to keep them at full speed. Sometimes I let my horse run as hard as he could, and at other times I reined him down to a lope. After the first few rounds the horses began to run in something like a circle. This was a great help to Gholson and me, for we would keep the inside of the circle and save a lot of distance. Gholson relieved me after about three hours, and by this time the mustangs were making a complete circle. We were having moonlight nights, so we had no trouble keeping up the chase at night. By the morning of the third day we had the horses so leg-weary we could drive them where we wished.

The leader of this band was a blood-bay stallion, untouched by human hand. He was game to the last, always taking the lead. When the herd began to show the effects of the long race, and several horses began to lag behind, he would leave his place in front and go back urging the lagging ones to greater speed. When milder tactics failed, he would turn on them, kicking and biting. When we started the herd the way we wanted to go, the leader would drop back and show fight. Sometimes he would run very close to us, arching his neck and showing his teeth. We developed a profound admiration for this stallion, but we concluded that the herd would never be manageable as long as he was in it, and the only way to get him out of it was to shoot him. About the hardest job I ever did was to kill this wonderful piece of horseflesh. We then had no trouble getting the rest of the mustangs to the Llano Corrals. We were dead tired when we got in; so we put them in the pens for the night.

The next morning we roped and hog-tied every horse in the herd. There were thirty-six in all; twelve of them had been branded. We found a pile of old horse shoes at the corrals; we placed a shoe on a horse's foreleg just above the pastern joint, and mashed the heels of the shoe together. This allowed the shoe to drop over the ankle and act as a clog to prevent the horse from running. We kept the mustangs under herd for several weeks, and then traded them to a professional horse dealer who shipped them to Louisiana to sell to cotton farmers. I have

often wondered how those mustangs acted in the
cotton patches of easy-going Louisiana. However, I
have heard that shipping a horse several hundred
miles on the railroad often takes the cussedness out
of the wildest outlaws.

During the 80's there were a few men, called
mustangers, who made their living by walking or
running down mustangs. If the mustangers rode
horses, they usually ran the mustangs down, and that
was much quicker. If the mustangers footed it, they
walked the horses down. That took from a week to
ten days. Two men could take time about and keep
continually on the move, never giving them a chance
to eat. They always started the marathon just before
the full of the moon, so as to have sufficient light at
nights. This method was slower than running, but it
caused the mustangs to be more gentle and easier to
control. The mustangers would work with the horses
a few weeks until they could handle them fairly
well, and then sell or trade them to some horse dealer. Two of the Hunt boys of Estacado, L. D. and
Roll, tamed several bunches of wild horses in this
way.

When I took charge of the Llano Ranch on August 1, 1883, the outfit had just got installed in the
new headquarters. A two-story frame house was just
being finished at the foot of the Caprock about three
miles southwest of where Post was later located.
Nearby were the new plank corrals, high and solid.

Along with Galbraith's job I had to take over his
troubles. A minor but an irritating one was friction

with the red-headed bookkeeper. No matter what I
did, it was not to his liking. If I gave an order for
a load of chuck, he would ride fifteen miles looking
for me to ask if I did not order too much of some
article, or if I could not get along without something else. He thought because he owned a few shares
of stock that he was a part of the company, and I
could not fire him. I put up with him three months,
and then made him leave the ranch.

The fencing was not yet finished. The south and
east lines were up and the men were working on the
north line. John W. Woody had the contract to fence
the entire ranch. The posts and stays were procured
from the cedar brakes west and south of Post.
Posts were hard to get, for the brakes were so rough
one could not get to the timber with a wagon. The
posts had to be snaked out with mules to where they
could be loaded on a wagon. Galbraith had helped to
get out the posts for the new corrals during the
spring and summer of 1883, and when he quit he had
huge callouses on his shoulders and hands.

Woody placed the posts every forty feet with three
stays to each panel. There were four wires tightly
stretched. The ranch was originally fenced with
barbed wire. The barbs were long with four points
and were close together. After the fence cutters
started getting in their work, the barbed wire was
partly replaced by ribbon wire; it had one barb about
every five inches, and was so heavy it could not be
cut with a pair of common pliers. The barb was not
twisted around the wire, but was a claw jutting out

from the ribbon. I never knew the exact cost of the Llano fence, for I had nothing to do with its construction except to inspect the north and west lines for the company after Woody had completed them.

If I didn't have anything to do with the fence's construction, I had a-plenty to do with its repair; for it was scarcely finished when the fence-cutters got busy again. Soon after I took charge of the outfit I began to get threatening anonymous letters from the free-rangers. They said they had always been my friends, but as I had taken Galbraith's place, I must leave the ranch or take the consequences. I knew pretty well whom the letters were from. I paid no attention to the threats and sent the free-rangers word that I would look after the interest of the Llanos as long as I was able to ride a horse.

I placed two men at riding fence (line-riding), and in a few days they came in and quit. They said they would not work at a job where they were shot at by parties from concealed places. They each had been shot at several times at long range with Winchesters. I put two more hands riding fence, and the next day they came in and quit for the same reason. Then I wrote Colonel Young a long letter explaining the situation. Before I could hear from Young the free-rangers did another job of fence-cutting on the north. For a mile they cut the wire on each side of the posts so that the wire could not be used again. Then they drove several thousand head of cattle through the gap into the pasture.

A few days later I received the following letter
from Colonel Young:

"I will have a man there next week to assist you in riding
the lines. Fix him up in good shape and ask no questions. Do
the best you can in this matter, and conduct the business in as
honorable and gentlemanly a way as possible."

When the man arrived I remembered having seen
him before. His name was Bill G——, and he had
been a peace officer at Fort Griffin during the time
when that town was the toughest place in the State.
He had two or three notches on his gun when he left
Fort Griffin in 1881. Then he went to Sweetwater,
where he added two more notches. Soon after he left
the Llano outfit he went back to Sweetwater, where
he was killed by another "tough one".

A few days later Young sent three other gunmen
to assist Bill G——. I had never seen them before,
but I found out later they all had "good records"
and "plenty of notches". The company was to furnish them with camp equipment and chuck, pay them
each a hundred dollars a month, and a bonus if
they killed a man in the act of cutting the fence. I
followed instructions by fixing them up a camp on
the north line and "asking no questions". I saw very
little of them the several months they were there.

The fence-cutting did not stop. In spite of the
gunmen, stretches of fence were repeatedly riddled
and outside cattle driven in. Cutting fence was not
the only damage the free-rangers were doing. They
were shooting and killing hundreds of Curry Comb
cattle. There were two reasons for this: first to in-

timidate us, and second, to rid the range of cattle which were eating the precious grass they coveted. We spent most of the winter rounding up their cattle and putting them outside, and repairing fence. I decided to put the cattle out of the pasture on the opposite side from their owner's ranges. That caused the free-rangers a lot of trouble.

Early in the spring of 1884 the Llano gunmen caught two fence-cutters in the act. They took a few long-range shots at them, but the fence-cutters managed to get away. The affair must have thrown a scare into the free-rangers, for a short time later several of them came to me and said that if I would disarm the line-riders, there would be no more fences cut. I told them I would not disarm the men, but assured them they would not be molested if they left the fence alone. This ended the fence-cutting, and soon afterwards Colonel Young let the gunmen go.

I gave one of the gunmen a job punchin' cattle. John was the only name we ever knew him by; no one was indiscreet enough to ask him if he had another. When I left the Llano Ranch and went to the Square and Compass, I took him with me. Two years later he went to Montana with a shipment of steers. He didn't come back, and I didn't hear of him for five years. Then I received a fine, handmade bridle and two dozen watch chains all made of horse hair. A note accompanying them instructed me to sell the articles, and send the money to the warden of the penitentiary at ———, Montana. The proceeds would go to Convict No.———. I always thought

this was John. I sold the bridle for $25 and the watch
chains for $1.50 each, and sent the money as directed.
Three months later I received two dozen watch
chains, but no bridle. The sale of the second shipment was slow, for the market was glutted. I finally
sold a dozen and sent the money to the warden. A
few weeks later the money was returned to me with a
letter stating that Convict No.——— was not there;
I never knew whether he died, escaped, or was
turned loose.

In the summer of 1884, I saw three coyotes run
down an antelope. As a rule, an antelope runs in a
straight line at first, but will eventually swing into a
wide circle as mustangs do. When I first saw the race
after coming over a ridge, the antelope was already
running in a circle, and one coyote was after him. I
stopped and watched the chase. In a little while the
coyote doing the running dropped out, and a second
coyote took up the chase. He made a circle or two,
and the third one relieved him. It was apparent that
the coyotes were using the same tactics on the antelope that men used on mustangs. The coyotes were
gaining on the antelope. The longer the chase lasted,
the smaller became the circle and the more distance
the coyotes could cut by keeping on the inside of the
circle. I sat on my horse and looked on for two hours
before the coyotes captured their prize. I did not
molest them. I thought that since they had used so
much sense in the chase they had earned their fresh
meat.

A few days later I saw a buzzard light on the rim

of the Caprock and disappear in a hole near the
edge. I figured there was a buzzard's nest in the cave;
and I had always wanted to see one. I tied my horse
and climbed the bluff. The hole was shallow, and
when I got up even with it I saw a mother buzzard
and two young buzzards. The young ones were the
ugliest things I had ever seen. When she saw me,
the old buzzard came to the edge of the cave and
began to flop her wings and vomit. I backed off and
wondered if vomiting was the way she had of defending her young. After she retired to the rear of
the cave I went a little closer. The old buzzard came
out and began to vomit at me again. It was the worst
smelling scent I ever came in contact with. After the
old buzzard made such a heroic defense of her young,
I left without taking a shot at her.

Since I have learned that vomiting is the buzzard's
only means of defense, but take my word for it, it is
effective. I am sure that no vermin with a sense of
smell would ever venture into a buzzard's nest. I
have seen lots of carcasses of buzzards and coyotes,
but I have never seen a single one that had been
molested by other vermin. I doubt seriously if there
is anything in the world that will eat a buzzard;
I am not so sure about coyotes.

We had a puncher on the ranch whom we called
Sam. He was a good fellow and a top hand, but he
had never heard of any rules of hygiene. He had
lots of hair on his body and was always dirty. He
brought a stock of lice with him to the ranch. The
lice spread in the bunk house and the other boys got

a supply. They got to where they would bet on louse fights. Two boys would get up a bet, each would catch a louse off his body, and place the combatants together on a slicker spread on the ground. The lice would fight, but the bets would usually have to be called off, because in the mix-up the identity of the lice would be lost and there was no way of telling whose louse won. However, both punchers would claim that the winner belonged to him.

I sent to Colorado City for two forty-gallon wash pots. I had the boys take all their clothes and bedding and boil them in these pots. At the same time I had the boys take baths with lots of lye soap. It took three general dippings to rid the place of lice. After that we made Sam take a bath and change clothes at least once every three months.

Sam thought a lot of me. He worked hard, saved his money, and had no relatives. He always said he intended to leave his money to me. After I left the Llanos he was manager for a month or so, but was too unlettered to handle the business. He couldn't go to town without getting on a spree. In 1891 he went to Colorado City, got on a big spree, and died in a house of prostitution. He had about $2,500 in the bank at the time. The prostitutes managed to get all his money before he died. While he was drunk they had him go to the bank and draw it out in $400 or $500 lots. Many people thought that he was a victim of foul play. His virtues and weaknesses were typical of a certain class of punchers.

In October, 1883, I went to Fisher County and

bought seventy-five unbroken saddle horses from Sol
Barron. Coming back through Scurry County, I struck
up with Jim McCommis and engaged him to come
to the Llano Ranch and break the Barron horses. Jim
was a likable, handsome fellow, tall, blue-eyed,
sandy-haired, with a short mustache. He was a big
success with the ladies, as was evidenced by the fact
that he got one to marry him at a time when there
were only two eligible young ladies in Dickens and
Crosby Counties and each one had a score or more
of suitors. In 1883 he married Della Browning.
When I made the trade with Jim about the horses,
it was agreed that his wife was to keep house at
headquarters and do the cooking when the wagon
cook was out on the range.

About four months after they came to the ranch,
Mrs. McCommis became faint one morning and began to feel the pains of child-birth. It was her first
time, and she was nervous and apprehensive about
it all. Jim was busting broncs at the corrals when
she went out and told him about it. It was eighty
miles to the nearest available doctor. It would take
him at least twenty-four hours to get there, provided
one could be found when the rider got to town.
Besides the pains were coming fast already.

The baby, a girl, was born without medical aid,
disinfectants, or anesthetics to alleviate the pain, and
with only the hard, clumsy hands of Jim to assist.
It died a few hours after it was born, a sacrifice to
frontier privations. The boys all came in and we got
things ready for the burial. John Hefker, the Ger-

man wagon cook, was a sort of carpenter and made
the coffin. He had to take some boards off the grain
house. The little coffin, a foot wide, a foot deep, and
two and a half feet long, was rough and we lined
the inside with a sheet. We dressed the baby in a
little white dress its mother had spent many hours
making months before, anxious, intent, wondering. It
was a pretty baby, not so red as most new-born in-
fants are, and when we placed it in its coffin, we had
a hard time to keep from breaking down. The boys
dug the grave between two cedar bushes northwest
of the house. They went to the creek and got six
large slabs of stone to make a vault for the coffin
in the bottom of the grave. They put one in the bottom for a floor; then roughly hewed four to make
the sides, and shaped one for the top.

Late in the afternoon we had everything ready
for the burial. Two cowboys carried the little coffin,
and the rest of us trailed along behind. Mrs. Mc-
Commis could not go. Things had gone badly with
her, and we still did not know whether she would
live or not. Jim left her a few minutes to come along
with us.

An open grave, a tiny coffin, and a dozen rough-
fisted, hardworking cowpunchers standing around
was all we had. We didn't have any singing, praying,
or speech-making. What we did was probably more
effective than that. We just placed the little coffin
in the rock vault and paused for a moment. Everything was awfully still, and there was moisture in
every puncher's eyes. Two or three were sniffling a

little bit, and big, hot tears were running down Jim's cheeks. Then we placed the slab of stone over the coffin, and filled the grave. This was the first birth and first burial in Garza county.

Mrs. McCommis' whole life was identified with the frontier. Two months after the burial of her baby, she started on a trek across the Plains, driving her own wagon behind a trail herd her husband was bossing. Jim was taking 3,500 J MIL cattle to New Mexico. The outfit had a four-horse chuck wagon, and Mrs. McCommis trailed along behind with a two-horse wagon containing everything that she and Jim owned. They went up the Yellow House, by Fort Sumner, and delivered the cattle to the Mill's Ranch on the upper Penasco River. In 1885 Jim was sent back to Scurry County to get another J MIL herd, and she trailed along behind him in her wagon, this time with a child to look after. Jim trailed this herd by way of Midland and Pecos. They were from October to the middle of January getting to the Penasco River. The last few days of the drive was made in snow two feet deep, Mrs. McCommis still driving her wagon, attending her child, and heavy with another.

She went on trailing after her husband, to New Mexico, to Texas, to Arizona, to California, a new child appearing every year or two, occasionally losing one. She had nineteen children and buried nine of them. Finally she buried Jim in Big Pine, California, in 1912. After her husband died the lure of the trail still called her. She took her seven youngest children and trekked back to New Mexico, where she is still living in the most primitive country left.

In May, 1884, I had a peculiar experience with lightning. We had been on a round-up at Yellow House Canyon just above Singer's Store. We started back with our herd and camped about eight miles below where Lubbock was later located. That night an electrical storm came up, and all hands turned out to help hold the cattle. I never before or since saw such a display of lightning. It commenced with flash lightning; then it became forked lightning; then chain lightning, followed by a peculiar blue lightning. After that show, it quickly developed into ball lightning, which rolled along the ground, and after that, spark lightning. You could see it on the horns of the cattle, on the ears of our horses, and the brims of our hats. Most extraordinary of all, the lightning settled down on us like a fog. The air smelled of burning sulphur. It grew so hot and sultry, we thought we would be burned. The cattle were extremely nervous until the storm passed about an hour later.

I had always thought that a vinegar-roan was extremely poisonous, but in June, 1884, I changed my mind about it. We were rounding-up in the Llano pasture. After breakfast one morning the cook started to empty the grounds out of the coffee pot, when he noticed a queer looking insect among the grounds. He called me (I was the only one left in camp) and asked what I thought it was. I told him it was a vinegar-roan. The cook got pale, and began to complain of feeling sick. Then he got panicky, and knew that all the boys would die. I figured that his ailment was purely imaginary, so I manufactured a lie for him.

"I was working with an outfit one time when the cook found a whole nest of vinegar-roans in the coffee grounds."

"Did the boys die?"

"No, it just gave them more pep."

That seemed to help the cook, and he was soon feeling better. I told him not to tell the boys, for they might run him out of camp. I also suggested that it would be a good idea to wash the coffee pot after each meal, and keep it covered up. The vinegar-roan juice did not seem to hurt any of the boys. A few days later I told them about the incident. Some of them "remembered" that they had felt puny that day, but others said they had never felt better and told the cook to put a vinegar-roan in the coffee every morning.

The Llano Company had made lots of enemies. The free-rangers on all sides were dogged, sullen, and abusive. As I was the manager and resident representative of the absentee owners who had dared to string wire with prickly barbs on it around the grass and water holes which belonged to free-rangers by divine right, it was I who received their maledictions. There were men who hated me cordially enough to have taken a pot shot at me if they had had sufficient opportunity. Aside from the physical aspect,

there was the social outlook. I was more or less iso-
lated. I couldn't hail and be jolly with most of my
neighbors. A friendly greeting would likely bring
forth a scowl. In July, 1884, I decided that the salary
I was getting was not worth the unpleasantness which
the position entailed, and sent my resignation to
President Young.

But times were changing fast. Barbed wire with
its sharp, pointed spikes was provoking a revolution
in the cattle business. Within two years practically
all of the free-rangers who had given me trouble
had to move their cattle on to New Mexico, and their
former ranges were acquired and fenced by cattlemen
and companies who had more vision than they.

CHAPTER XI

THE SQUARE AND COMPASS RANCH

THE week I resigned as manager of the Llano
Cattle Company I started negotiations with the Nave-
McCord Cattle Company in regard to the managership of the Square and Compass, $\bowtie$, Ranch.
Colonel Young wrote a strong recommendation, and
this together with the fact that Mr. Nave had known
my father during the 50's in Missouri, secured me
the place. The same day I left the Llano Ranch I
took charge of the Square and Compass outfit.

Abram Nave and James McCord were wholesale
grocers at Saint Jo, Missouri. They had wholesale
houses in Saint Jo, Omaha, Denver and Kansas City.
When cattle prices began to soar during the early
80's, they decided to invest their surplus in the cattle
ranching business. In 1882 they bought 1,500 head
of cattle, and the range rights of Jim and Finis
Lindsey on the Double Mountain River at the mouth
of Spring Creek, Garza County. They bought more
cattle from George B. Loving in Jack County. For
a number of years they built up the size of their herd
by retaining all the heifers.

From the outset they started a policy of acquiring
the land where their cattle ranged. By 1884 they had
purchased and leased a tract eighteen miles north and
south and twelve miles east and west, with a range
capacity of about twelve thousand cattle. The ranch
lay directly south of the Llanos with the west line
reaching about three miles farther west than the
Llano west line. About half of the land was on
the Plains and about half in the breaks east of the
Caprock. This made a desirable location. The broken
country made a good winter pasture, and in the summer no finer grass was to be found anywhere than
on the Plains.

The headquarters was located between the Caprock and Double Mountain River[1] near the present
headquarters of the John L. Slaughter estate. The
main house had two large frame rooms and porch in
front with two long shed rooms behind used as dining
room and kitchen. Nearby was a bunk house, sixteen
by thirty. The corrals, when I took charge, were made
of rock against the Caprock on the south side. They
were constructed in such a way that in the afternoon
cattle had to be driven in against the sun. For some
reason it is very difficult to pen cattle against the sun.

------

[1]There has been some confusion as to the identity of the
Double Mountain River. Some maps show Yellow House Creek
as the upper Double Mountain. Historically, the upper Double
Mountain is the prong which rises in Lynn County in what is
locally known as Mooar's Draugh and runs through the southern
part of Garza County and makes a junction with Yellow House
Creek in Kent County, about fifteen miles southwest of Claire-
mont.

One of the first things I did was to have lumber hauled from Colorado City and new plank corrals made with approaches from the south.

In the fall of 1884 Nave and McCord made a reorganization in the ranch management. From the beginning they had an official called general manager, who had an office at Fort Worth, and spent most of his time there. This position was held by a man named Z——. Occasionally, Z—— would come to Colorado City for a few days, and more rarely would pay the ranch a flying visit. He was a northern man and knew little about cattle. About two months after I became the ranch manager Mr. Nave sent word to both Z— and myself to meet him in Colorado City. When he arrived he found Z—— had registered at the Saint James Hotel, but was not to be found. Mr. Nave soon ran across me, and together we went to look for Z——. At last we located him, drunk, in a house of prostitution. Mr. Nave promptly fired Z— and abolished the position of general manager. Thereafter I had all my relations directly with the company at Saint Jo.

By this time Nave and McCord had decided the time had come to start fencing. Since they had a legal title to their land, two substantial benefits would accrue from inclosing the range; they could better handle their own cattle and do it with fewer men, and they could better prevent outsiders from making use of their grass. The company bought half interest in the Llano fence on the north side of the Square and Compass range, and let a contract for the construction of the other three sides. The contractor did the south line first, the west line next, and the east line last.

He procured posts from the cedar brakes east of the Caprock, and set them in the line every sixty feet. The Llanos put posts at forty feet, but experience showed that sixty-foot spans were better than forty-foot ones. The longer panels allowed more give, and an animal was not so apt to break the wire when he hit the fence. Three stays were placed between each set of posts. Wire cost three dollars a hundred at Colorado City plus the price of hauling, which was sixty cents a hundred. The distance from Colorado City was sixty-five miles. The total cost of the fence was approximately $100 a mile.

When the contractor finished his job, I inspected and accepted the fence. It was necessary for us to go to Colorado City to make settlement. We stopped at the Saint James Hotel, I figured out what was due him, and gave him a check. He was perfectly satisfied with the amount. After supper I ran over my figures again and found I had made a mistake of forty-odd dollars in the company's favor. I went out to look for the man and found him half drunk in a saloon. I told him I had made a mistake, and if he would come to the hotel next morning I would make the correction. He promised to be there promptly at nine o'clock. I have never seen the man to this day. He probably thought the mistake was in his favor and that I had overpaid him.

In July, 1884, I rode over one morning to the

Jumbo headquarters to see if any mail had been left there for us. If anyone from that ranch went to Colorado he brought out mail for all the neighbors, and when any of us went to town we did the same. In this way we usually managed to get the mail about every two or three weeks. When I got to the Jumbo Ranch the men were all away on a round-up. Mrs. Palmer, the housekeeper, came running out to tell me there was a very sick puncher in the bunk house. He had been up there "reping" for the "Lum" Slaughter outfit, and had gotten so sick three days before he had to come in and go to bed.

I went to the bunk house and, at a glance, I knew he was in a critical condition. I told him that he had better let us send him to the nearest doctor at Snyder at once. He agreed, and I hurried back to the Square and Compass headquarters for our two-horse hack. I thought I would send a man to drive the hack, but there was not a man on the place, and I didn't think it wise to take the time to go and find one. I put a pair of springs and a mattress in the back of the hack and went back as fast as I could to get the sick man. It was noon when we got started to Snyder, forty miles away. I wanted to drive through without stopping.

In the afternoon the man got delirious and violent; I had to tie him to his bed. I knew time was getting precious and I kept watching the sun. I remembered how an old gentleman—I believe his name was Joshua—had commanded the sun to stand still, and I wished I might be able to do some commanding

myself. There was only one house on the road to
Snyder; it was on the bank of Gavitt Creek and was
occupied by a family by the name of Knowles. I was
hoping I would be able to get someone there to go
on to Snyder and help me care for the sick man. An
electrical storm came up about dark just before I
got to Knowles', and it soon got so dark I could not
see the road except when the lightning flashed. When
I got to Knowles' there was no one there except Mrs.
Knowles and five small children. I thought of going
on alone but Mrs. Knowles said the creek had just
come down bank full and could not be crossed.

There was nothing to do but spend the night. I
got the sick puncher in the house, and then had to
hold him on the bed all night. He moaned, yelled,
prayed and rolled. I was tired to start with and next
morning I felt like I had been a week in a mad house.
Mrs. Knowles kept the coffee pot on the stove all
night and I had drunk a half gallon of strong, black
coffee. By daylight the creek had run down and I
got the man in the hack and started on.

When I got to Snyder I carried the puncher to the
little, one-horse hotel, and the people would not take
him in unless I would guarantee to pay the expense.
I hustled the doctor, and he would not have anything
to do with the case unless I promised to be responsible. I obligated myself for all expenses and
left the puncher in the doctor's care. Three hours
after I left, he died. The doctor said he had inflammation of the bowels, but it was probably appendicitis. Physicians did not seem to know anything

about appendicitis in those days, and pronounced such cases "inflammation of the bowels" and let the patient die. Had surgery been more highly developed then, the man's life might have been saved by a timely operation.

In October, 1884, we drove a beef herd of 1,600 steers to Colorado City. We carried along a wagon and a crew of eight men. The first night we camped in the Jumbo pasture; the second night, on Bull Creek in the Magnolia, or M K range; the third night, on Bull Creek in the Triangle H Triangle range, and the fifth day we watered on Deep Creek, near Colorado City. We had to hold the herd a few days because we could not get cars. After we loaded out, I turned the boys loose for the customary two nights and a day. On the second day we headed back for the ranch, a two-day trip going back.

As soon as the fall work was done in November, 1884, I left the ranch on a most important mission. I was going to get married. I left my team and hack at Mooar Brothers' livery stable at Colorado City and took the train to Gatesville.

My fiancée, Miss Mary Emma Boles, was thirteen when her family moved from Illinois in 1877 to Denison in Grayson County. The family settled near my father's place. I had seen her a few times, and the last time I visited my family I went to see her once or twice. In 1882 we got to writing to each other. In the meanwhile her family moved to Coryell County and settled near Gatesville. Our courtship was conducted almost entirely by correspondence.

Once I paid a negro five dollars to go to Estacado for
a letter, and when he got there he found none. We
kept all our love letters until our house burned in
1915. For over thirty years of my married life, every
time I did something Mrs. Burns did not like, she
could produce those old letters and show me what
I had promised. Since 1915, however, she has been
without documentary evidence as to my courting
declarations. When we were married, we left immediately for Colorado. There we purchased a few
household articles and started for the ranch in the
hack. It took two days to make the trip.

For awhile Mrs. Burns was the only woman in
Garza County. There had been four others, Mrs.
Laura Cooper, Mrs. Jim McCommis, Mrs. Captain
Hall, and a Mrs. Wescott, but they had all left the
county. Soon afterwards I got a man and his wife at
headquarters to cook and do general work. A few
months later Nick Beal, manager of the Jumbo, or
Buckle B ⦿B Ranch, whose headquarters was six
miles south of ours, brought his wife out. A short
time after that Mr. and Mrs. Coon Cooper returned
and began working on the Llano Ranch. That made
five women in the county. The next spring George
and Will Boles, my wife's brothers, came out and
started working on the Square and Compass as cowboys. This kept Mrs. Burns from getting so lonesome
in a country where the nearest neighbors were six
miles away.

Late in the fall of 1884 there were several days
of cold rain and sleet from the northeast. All over

West Texas cattle started drifting southwest. They did the most of their moving at night, and the ranchmen were not aware of the enormity of the drift until the spell of weather was over. Cattle on the Plains drifted off the Caprock to the southwest in New Mexico. A great number of the cattle in our country went to the Pecos River. Our range was full of Matador and Spur cattle from the northeast.

There was no chance of getting the cattle back before spring. In March over twenty ranchmen sent wagon outfits to the Pecos country. I sent a wagon with Pete McSpadden as boss, an extra puncher, a cook, and a wrangler. Eight stray cowboys (men from ranches that had not sent wagons) were attached to our wagon. When all the outfits got to the Pecos, there were so many they could not effectively work without organization. Somebody sent word around for all bosses to meet in a consultation. Gus O'Keefe, from the "Lum" Slaughter ranch, was elected general superintendent.

A general round-up was held, and no attempt was made to separate the cattle. Each outfit was given a herd of mixed cattle to drive to the head of Colorado River where the cattle were again concentrated and separated. There were only two watering places between the Pecos and the Colorado. The cattlemen had to arrange with the Texas and Pacific Railroad to haul water for a third watering. Over 30,000 cattle were driven east of the Colorado. Practically the entire calf crop in the drift was lost. This experience caused many ranchmen to think more seriously about fencing their ranges.

In February I had heard that a number of Square and Compass cattle were in the Cedar Lake country in Gaines County. About the time McSpadden's outfit started for the Pecos, I took another wagon and set out for Cedar Lake. The third day out, as we were approaching the lake, I was riding my top horse, Tallow Eye, behind the *remuda*. Four of the boys were riding half a mile in front of the wagon and *remuda*. Suddenly I heard shots and yelling, and looked up to see the boys chasing nine grown buffaloes. They were coming quartering in my direction. I had a Winchester on my saddle, and it didn't take long to get alongside an old cow. I brought her down the second shot. The other boys were much disappointed in not getting a buffalo, but I had the advantage; Tallow Eye was fast and not afraid of a buffalo, and their horses were. So far as I know, this was the last wild buffalo killed on the South Plains.

We took the hide and meat from the buffalo and went on to "One Arm" Anderson's place on the north end of the lake, where there were some fresh water springs. Anderson was at camp, and I told him I had killed a buffalo. He gave me a sour and disconcerting look and said, "You have killed one of my tame buffaloes."

"But this buffalo was a wild one."

"I captured six calves last year. They are now

yearlings, and the only buffaloes left in this country."

"Well, Mr. Anderson, if your buffaloes were yearlings, the one I killed was not yours, for she was an old cow."

Then we brought out the hide and showed him. He apologized and became quite friendly. He told us that an outfit from the I O A, or Cross C Ranch, in Lubbock County, had rounded up the Cedar Lake country, and had taken all strays from the north and east back with them. Next morning he gave me one of his yearling buffaloes. I told him I could not take it with me but I would come after it sometime during the year. He later sent me word to come and get the buffalo, but I never did go.

The next morning I started the outfit to the I O A Ranch, and I took a chunk of the buffalo meat and went directly home. My wife and several of the punchers at the ranch had never tasted buffalo meat, so the piece I carried home was quite a novelty.

A short time later the ranch owners of Northwest Texas (not including the Panhandle) met in Abilene and organized the general spring round-ups. They divided the country into three districts. One included the region drained by the Colorado River and its tributaries from Colorado City to the Plains; the second, the Double Mountain and Salt Forks of the Brazos from the east Kent County line west, together with the upper Pease region, and the third district lay east of the second. The ranchmen of each district elected a general superintendent, who was to receive five dollars a day for the duration of the work. He was to have full charge of all wagons and men— twelve to fifteen wagons with from ten to fifteen men each. Any one not obeying the superintendent was to be discharged by his manager. The superintendent was to consult with the manager of each range as to the best way to work it.

When the cattlemen of the Double Mountain and Salt Fork district met to elect their superintendent, Colonel Young addressed the meeting: "There is a man in this audience who has the ability and courage for this important position. He was manager of our ranch (Llanos) and is now manager of the Square and Compass. I nominate Rollie Burns."

I was elected without opposition. I thanked the ranchmen, and told them I was sure my employers would not like for me to be away for sixty days at one time, but that I would appoint an assistant superintendent, and give as much of my time to the matter as possible. This was satisfactory.

When the round-up began, I appointed Dick Palmer, wagon boss for the Matadors, as assistant superintendent. Dick made a good executive, and when I received my check from the association I endorsed it and sent it on to him. Next spring I was elected general superintendent again, and appointed Henry Ramsey, wagon boss for an outfit in Scurry County; he made good. In the spring of 1887 I was elected for a third time, and appointed Boley Brown as assistant. He proved to be very satisfactory. That was the last year of the general round-up. The country was pretty well fenced up by that time, and cattle could not stray from their ranges as they had before. After 1887, round-ups became local affairs. Each ranch held its own round-ups, and the neighboring ranches sent men to "rep" for them.

In the summer of 1885 we had a rather serious stampede of our saddle horses. The horse pasture contained about four sections. The Caprock made the north and west boundaries, and there was a four-wire fence on the south and east sides. It was a foggy day, and the horses were over on the west side. A black bear came down the Caprock near the horses and gave them a tremendous scare. They ran across the horse pasture, struck the east fence, tore it down, and ran for miles in the big pasture. When we got them rounded up, we found thirty-eight out of a hundred and forty were badly cut. I sewed the wounds up with a surgeon's needle and linen thread, which we always kept on hand. One horse was hopelessly cut and had to be killed. No one saw the bear at the time, but one had been seen the day before, and we found where he had come down the Caprock near where the stampede began.

While riding along Gavitt Creek on my way to spend a few days with the general round-up during the summer of 1885, I saw an eagle about a mile off flying in a circle and making peculiar maneuvers. He would drop to the ground and then rise again. I concluded he was trying to catch something, and I turned in his direction to see what it was. Closer I saw he was after a young deer. I stopped my horse to watch the performance. The eagle would dip down and catch the deer with both claws in the loins just in front of the hips, and turn the deer heels over head. The third time the deer was thrown it did not try to get up. I suppose it was tired and exhausted. The eagle then lit on the ground and began to peck out the eyes of the deer. At this point I decided to interfere, put spurs to my horse and dashed over the intervening two hundred yards. I presume the bird was too busy thinking about the good eats of juicy venison he was about to have to keep his eagle eye on anything other than his prey. I was within twenty feet of him before he saw me. I fired two shots with my six-shooter before he could take off, and broke his wing. A third shot finished him, and then I turned to the deer. The eagle had destroyed one eye. I lifted it on its feet, and it ran off in a zig-zag way on account of losing the eye.

About a year later I witnessed a similar occurrence on the Square and Compas Ranch. This time the eagle was after a young calf. I was quite a distance off when I saw the eagle throw the calf head over heels. By the time I got there the eagle had both eyes pecked out, and had begun to peck a place in the calf's flank where the hide is thinnest and nearest to the calf's entrails. That is the eagle's method— to peck out the eyes and disembowel his prey before the victim is dead. I took a shot at the bird, but missed.

At the time eagles were injuring and killing many calves, especially in the breaks just off the Caprock.

I instructed all the cowboys to kill an eagle every
chance they got. We found a roosting place on the
head of Double Mountain Fork, about ten miles
above our headquarters. We made a number of raids
up there at night and killed many eagles.

During the 80's and 90's I experienced a number
of "blue northers," but the bluest of them all was
in January, 1886. I left Colorado City for the ranch
on January 13, about ten o'clock in the morning. It
was a beautiful day, clear, still, warm. I was riding
my top horse, Tallow Eye, a fine, gaited saddle horse
as well as a good cow horse. I enjoyed the first five or
six miles of the ride, and then I noticed a blue streak
low down in the far north. I knew what it meant.
I think "Tallow Eye" noticed it about the time I did,
for he began to get nervous and wanted to go faster.
I kept watching the blue streak and saw it was rising
fast. Tallow Eye was getting excited, and a slight
touch with my spurs was sufficient signal for him to
speed up. In a mile or two we overtook a buggy
going in the same direction. The driver was Bayless
Wagoner, manager of the Triangle H Triangle
Ranch, owned by the Alabama and Texas Cattle
Company. I asked Wagoner what he thought of the
blue streak. He said it was a "blue swishler" dead
sure, and for me to tie my horse to the side of his
horses and get in the buggy. We could both get under
his lap-robe, and by driving fast we ought to get to
the Triangle H Triangle before it got very cold.

It was about ten miles to the ranch, but we had
not gone over a mile when the norther was on us.

It hit us with a force that almost upset the buggy, and
the wind was icy. I am confident that we had zero
weather within ten minutes. Wagoner put the horses
in a gallop and occasionally in a run. We were not
over forty-five minutes getting to the ranch, but we
were almost stiff when we got there. We drove up
on the south side of the house and called to the boys
to come take the horses. We were so numb the boys
had to help get us into the house.

There was a big box stove in the center of the
room, and the boys had it full of good mesquite
wood. The stove was red hot, but it thawed us out
slowly. The house was badly built to keep out cold
weather. The floor was a foot from the ground, and
the house had no underpinning. There were cracks
in the floor and the wind rushed through. The house
was a good summer house, but not so much in the
winter. Not one of the six of us pretended to go to
bed. We hugged the stove all night. It was too cold
for a game of cards or a yarn.

When daylight came, the cook went out to cut
some beef for breakfast. The beef had been hanging
from the windmill tower all night and was frozen
hard. He came back and reported that he couldn't
cut any meat, and we would have to eat breakfast
without any steak. I told Wagoner to tell the cook
to lay the meat on the ground and chop off some
hunks of steak with the axe.

After breakfast I told Wagoner I must get on towards home. The weather had not abated a bit, but
I had a wife and baby and twelve thousand cattle I

wanted to see about. I thought that if I could get twenty-five miles to the Magnolia Ranch that day, I would be able to get home the next. We had to face the wind all day. We would trot, lope, and occasionally go in a dead run. When Tallow Eye began to get tired I would walk and lead him until I got tired. When we got to the Magnolia Ranch, Jack Rogers, the manager, saw me before I got to the house. He ran out and helped me to dismount. By this time I was almost stiff, notwithstanding I had on heavy woollen socks, clothing, and overcoat.

The Magnolia ranch house was better built than the Triangle H Triangle headquarters, and could be heated more easily. That night Rogers put me to bed in a room reserved for the "high-ups" from Kentucky. I had not slept for two days and a night, and that night I made up for it. The next morning the cook went to the well to get water for breakfast, and found the water twenty feet below the surface frozen over. It was a dug well about three or four feet in diameter. The cook had to put a heavy weight on the end of a lariat to break the ice.

That day Tallow Eye and I made the last lap to the Square and Compass by noon. I found my wife and baby all right, although they had had trouble keeping warm with all the wood they could burn. My wife's brother, George Boles, had been there keeping fires going. George said he had killed an antelope when the blizzard struck and was just fixing to skin it. The hide froze before he could finish, and he had to quit.

I was anxious to find out how the cattle were standing the driving cold. I asked the boys if they had
been to the southwest corner of the pasture, and found
that they had not. I knew that all the cattle on the
Plains had drifted there, so I took a couple of hands
and rode to the southwest corner. We found about
a thousand head congregated there, and about four
hundred were already dead or practically dead. We
drove the remainder off the Caprock into the breaks,
but the most of them were frozen so badly their
hoofs later dropped off and many died. Altogether,
I figured the direct and indirect losses due to this
blizzard were about 1,500, or about fifteen per cent
of the entire herd. Since that experience I am always
glad when January 13 is past.

Nick Beal, manager of the Jumbo Cattle Company, and I had a way of coöperating on outside
work. One time I would send a wagon and four men
and he would send four men; that made a workable
crew. Next time he would send a wagon and four
men and I would just send four men. In the spring
of 1886 we had sent an outfit to represent us at the
round-ups in the Colorado River country. The outfit
had worked several days and had accumulated quite
a herd of our strays when an electrical storm came
up during the night. Lightning and thunder cause
more stampedes than anything else. Cattle become
frantic, and their only thought seems to be to get
away from the horrifying display and the noise. That
night our herd was scared and restless, and all hands
were out trying to hold them. One of the Jumbo

punchers and the mulatto horse wrangler happened
to be close together when a bolt of lightning came
down, and hit them both. It killed the puncher and
his horse instantly. The mulatto fell in a puddle of
water, and I suppose that must have saved his life.
The crown of his hat was torn away, and there was
a blue welt down his back. The bolt of lightning
went from him through his horse and killed the
horse. That experience made the other six men along
afraid of electrical storms ever after that.

The year of 1886 was a dry one. Cattle everywhere suffered from lack of grass and water. If the
elements lack moisture they seem to be surcharged
with electricity. Practically every cloud had a violent
electrical display with little or no rain. A short time
after the two men in our outfit were struck, two
punchers in another outfit on the same work were
killed by lightning. That fall we were driving a beef
herd to Colorado City, when one of those violent
little clouds gathered to the west of us. In a few
moments the streaked lightning began to make an
almost continuous display, and thunder was sharply
clashing on the hills to the west; the cloud was coming in our direction. Some of the boys had been in
the Colorado River round-ups the previous spring
when the men were killed, and I had heard them say
they would not stay with any herd of cattle when a
bad electrical storm was on. I left my watch, ring
and spurs at the wagon and went out and told the
boys to go to the wagon and I would hold the herd
the best I could. They all went, and I never felt

more like leaving a herd and going myself. With every flash of lightning and roar of thunder I felt a little yellow streak in me. Each roar caused cattle to run by me. Fortunately, the storm was quickly over, and we had not gone over two miles when the boys overtook us. They began to make apologies and excuses for leaving the herd, but I told them I did not blame them, and for a little more I would have left myself.

In August, 1886, the first election was held in Garza County. The county was attached to Scurry, and we participated in the election of Scurry County officers, as well as state officials. I was appointed Presiding Officer of Elections of Precinct Number 1. That precinct included the whole county. The polls were at our headquarters, and about twelve or fifteen voted. That included all eligible voters from the Square and Compass, the Llanos, and the Coopers, and some small cattlemen in the east side of the county.

The drouth of 1886 caused a shortage of stock water on our range. Prior to that time the Square and Compass had depended on natural watering places. The Double Mountain Fork, which traversed the ranch from west to east, always had holes of water in it which had never before gone dry, and there were a number of spring creeks which rose at the Caprock and flowed into the Double Mountain. During the summer of 1886 nearly all the springs and water holes dried up. I had to keep several men busy scraping holes in the sandy bed of the river with teams and scrapers. The water would rise in these holes for a foot or so. We managed to keep sufficient water for the cattle, but the experience demonstrated the need for more watering facilities. That fall and winter I induced the owners to build two large tanks on arroyos in the breaks of the big pasture and a small tank on a little spring draugh in the horse pasture. We bored three wells on the Plains in the north part of the pasture and got an abundance of water at about a hundred and twenty feet. We put windmills over these wells and had that part of the pasture pretty well cared for. But we were not so fortunate with two wells in the southwest part of the pasture. We bored nearly three hundred feet and got scarcely any water at all in one, and barely enough in the other to furnish a line camp. The maximum capacity of the camp was one cowboy and four horses. However, with the tanks and the other three wells we never had another serious water shortage.

In the spring of 1887 I had a spell of sickness which came well nigh getting me. The second day my family sent to Snyder for a doctor, who came and stayed sixteen days and nights. He pronounced my malady inflammation of the bowels. The doctor gave me up three or four times, but I fooled him and lived. I have described my condition and symptoms to several physicians since, and they have all been of the opinion that I had appendicitis, and that my appendix burst. For days I vomited a substance as black as ink and of the vilest odor. I am sure it was my robust constitution that enabled me to throw the poison out of my system. The sickness caused the insides of my intestines to peel off, and they became as thin as paper. The doctors told me it would be five years before I could ride a horse, but in two years I was riding as much as ever.

While I was sick our second baby was born. When the first child came two years before, I carried my wife to Colorado a month before hand, and she had excellent care. She was not willing to leave me for the birth of the second child. It was impossible to get a doctor when she became ill, and the borning was without any kind of medical aid. The result was that I almost lost both my wife and the baby.

When this child was a little over a year old we had a close call with him. Water was scarce on the range and I had been having the creek beds scraped. We missed the children one day and my wife sent me in search of them. I went to a tree where they had last been seen playing. From there I tracked them to the creek a mile and a half away. When I got there I saw Lynn's little body floating face downward in the water of one of the holes the boys had scraped. His face was black when I took him out. I did everything I knew to restore a drowned person. I felt like I could not take the child back to its mother without life in it. Finally, I gave up, gathered him in my arms, and started to the house. I met my wife coming. She displayed more restraint and resourcefulness than most men would have under the circumstances. She said there was yet hope, and we set to work again. She told me to take him by the heels and shake him; I did, and a quantity of water ran out of his mouth. Then we went to the house and put him in hot water. A half hour after I had given up hope, he began to breathe again. I have always ascribed the saving of the child to the level-headedness of my wife.

I had been with the Square and Compass Ranch four years and three months, when I was offered the managership of the I O A, or Cross C Ranch in Lubbock County. The I O A outfit had about twice the land and cattle that the Square and Compass had, and the salary was higher. I accepted the place and took charge of the outfit December 11, 1888.

CHAPTER XII

THE I O A RANCH

THE Western Land and Live Stock Company was organized in 1884, at Davenport, Iowa, under the laws of Iowa, with a capital stock of $800,000. The company was made up of men residing in Davenport, and Moline, Illinois. J. S. Keater was the president, but the active management was largely in the hands of the vice-president, S. W. Wheelock. Mr. Wheelock was the president of the Moline National Bank, the Moline Plow Company, the Moline Wagon Company, and the Moline Paper Company.

The Western Land and Live Stock Company, wishing to do things in the approved way, established a Texas officer at Fort Worth and installed therein David Boaz, one of the directors, as general superintendent. It was Boaz's business to purchase land and cattle and start the ranch off. Boaz decided that Yellow House Canyon, in Lubbock County, was the most likely place still available. He started buying and leasing land with the vigor of a man who wanted to get started in the cattle business in a hurry. Within two years he had purchased or leased approximately

the south half of Lubbock County. The tract averaged fourteen by thirty miles, and included about
four hundred and twenty sections. Among other
lands he had leased the three sections in the old
Williams sheep ranch along the Yellow House, and
Williams' house became the headquarters of the new
ranch.

The land was partially watered by Yellow House
Creek, and Boaz hurried to get ten wells bored and
ten windmills erected. In the meanwhile he was
stocking the range with cattle. Cattle were high, and
Boaz allowed cattlemen who knew how to sell to
tenderfoot buyers to charge him more than the cattle
were worth. He bought 20,000 head at prices never
again reached until the Spanish-American War—an
outlay of a half million dollars.

In the meanwhile he was having the land fenced.
Posts had to be hauled for fifty miles, and wire from
Colorado. Two cross-fences were put in, cutting the
range into the West, Middle, and East pastures. In
all there were a hundred miles of fence, which cost
the company approximately $15,000. There had to
be saddle horses, and he bought two hundred for
$8,000.

When he had started stocking the range with cattle,
Boaz installed J. K. Millwee as ranch manager.
Millwee had worked for John Chissum in Lincoln
County, New Mexico, before Billy the Kid had
started the Lincoln County War. He had been a trail
boss, and was considered as good as any who drove
herds to Colorado and Kansas.

Nearly all of the directors of the company lived in Iowa. Local patriotism caused them to incorporate the "Iowa Motif" in their Texas ranch; hence, the brand was I O A (pronounced I-O-Wa when said fast). The "A" was what was called an "open A," made thus ∧ This brand was placed on the original 20,000 stock cattle. Millwee was not long in finding that Northern business men who tilted back in their swivel chairs in Davenport were most fallible when they came to adopting a brand. A brand could hardly have been selected that would have offered greater opportunities for changing by cattle thieves. It could easily be burned into . . .

ᒍOᴧ   ᕼOᴎ   IOᐱ   ꓔOᴧᴧ   ᴎOᴧ   ᕼOᴧ

and a score of other variations. During 1885 and 1886 thieves found good pickings on the I O A range. It was a common trick for an aspiring, would-be cowman with a maverick-hungry rope to file on a section of school land hardby the I O A pasture, build a shack, and register a brand that the I O A brand could be readily changed to. If he could burn the brand of a cow and brand a maverick or two a week, he would soon be getting on. It was customary for the I O A outfit to give some of the adjoining nesters a round-up. It was also customary for all the mavericks found on a particular man's range during a round-up to be branded with that person's brand. Some of the I O A's rustler neighbors were so brazen they scoured the adjoining country for mavericks just before the round-up reached them, and drove them at night to their range. When the round-up was held on their places, these imported mavericks were branded with their brands, and nothing could have given them a better title.

In 1886 the I O A Company purchased 1,500 cattle, branded Cross C Ɔ from Brigham Brothers who had been ranging for a year or two on Yellow House Creek just east of the present site of Lubbock. On Millwee's recommendation the company dropped the I O A brand and adopted the Cross C. This brand was hard to change, and thieves gave it a wide birth. The I O A cattle were gradually sold off, and by the time I took charge of the ranch in December, 1888, there were not many left; but the ranch continued to be known as the I O A Ranch.

After I became manager in 1888, some up-and-coming nesters, trying to get a start, branded a good many calves belonging to I O A cows on the north and east sides of our range. We reduced their activities to a minimum by keeping a close watch. I had a pretty good idea who the thieves were, but was never able to get sufficient evidence to warrant legal proceedings.

In 1890 and 1891 a band of rustlers became rather daring on the South Plains. They would steal a carload of beeves from several ranches, drive the cattle to railroad points not generally used for shipping, and ship them to some place where there were no inspectors, and sell to local butchers. In July, 1891, I received a letter from a lawyer in Arkansas who had lived in this region for several years and was familiar with the brands here. He said that several car loads of cattle from the South Plains had been shipped to Arkansas and sold to butchers. Among the cattle were several Cross C steers. I was sure that none of the cattle we had sold had been shipped to Arkansas. A short time later, several reliable persons in Amarillo sent me word that a certain butcher there had slaughtered several of our cattle. I sent the information to the sheriff of Potter County, but he wrote me that he was unable to find out anything about the matter.

I O A cattle had drifted badly during the winter of 1886. A thousand or more had gone as far as the Texas and Pacific Railroad, and some of them had never been brought back. In April, 1889, I sent a wagon, three punchers, a cook, and a wrangler to the Colorado, Big Spring, Midland country, to work the round-ups and gather our strays. Six or eight cowboys representing neighboring ranches went along to finish making up our crew. After this outfit had worked the round-ups along the Texas and Pacific Railroad, it started working back towards the home ranch, bringing our strays along. Even though many of the cattle had been strayed for three years, the boys brought back more cattle than originally drifted because of the increase.

All honest and legitimate cowmen branded the offspring of a stray with the brand of the mother. This was invariably the practice at regular round-ups. With many ranches represented, no one would have dared do otherwise. Occasionally a mistake was made, but was corrected through a policy of com-

pensation. For instance, in the jumble of a round-up
on the Slaughter range a Cross C calf might get
separated from its mother. The calf would be
branded with the Long S. Later the mistake would be
discovered. The Slaughter boss would then direct
that a calf following a Long S cow be branded Cross
C. In February, 1889, I received a letter from the
manager of the X I T Ranch apprising me of the
fact that five calves had been branded Cross C during
their round-ups during the previous year.

Notwithstanding the fact that this was the practice
of honest cowmen and regular round-ups, lots of
things could happen to strays. No outfit was as interested in the welfare of a stray as its own cattle. A
rustler could place his brand upon the calf of a stray
cow or change the brand of a stray animal with much
less risk than he could an animal which belonged on
that range. Many cow outfits made a practice of killing strays for beef. Somehow, stray meat was juicier,
sweeter, and more palatable.

While the wagon outfit was away to the south I
had a dozen punchers "reping" for us at the round-
ups to the east, north, and west. Cattle did not drift
north in the winter, but a few usually wandered off
in that direction during the spring, summer and fall.
Each year several of our cattle were found as far
north as the T Anchor range in the vicinity of Canyon
City.

The outside work usually lasted about two months.
About June the wagon outfit and the individual
"repers" got in, and then we began work on our

range. There was branding, marking, castrating and spaying to be done.

We had two chuck wagons, a small two-horse wagon, and a large four-horse wagon. When we worked our own range, and did not have any stray punchers (cowboys "reping" for other ranches), we used the two-horse wagon. On outside work and when we had heavy work at home with several stray men, we used the four-horse wagon. In the rear end of each wagon was a chuck-box in which we carried the grub. By the late 80's our grub had improved considerably as compared to what we had had on the "22" outfit a few years before. Now besides flour, coffee and salt, we had sugar, beans, dried fruits and canned goods. I never heard of canned goods being used on the range prior to 1884. In that year "Lum" Slaughter introduced them, and the use was soon taken up by other ranchmen. By 1889 most all of the larger outfits were furnishing their men with lots of good grub. The Square and Compass had fed unusually well. The owners were wholesale grocers, and seemed to take a peculiar pleasure in sending down shipments of food containing fancy eatables as well as staples. It was not unusual for them to send such items as pickled pig-feet and the like. The I O A Company did not furnish any fancy groceries, but they provided plenty of staples, and for meat we killed a yearling every two or three days.

Fuel for cooking and heating branding irons was a problem on the I O A Ranch. On the Llano and the Square and Compass we had used mesquite and cedar wood, but on the I O A we had to use cow-chips. It was harder to get a fire started with them, but when dry they made a hot fire. Although they gave off a peculiar odor when burning, this did not affect the food a particle. The cook always kept a quantity of chips in the "cooney" (a cow-hide swung hammock-like under the wagon) to keep them dry.

We had several corrals located in various parts of the pasture at different windmills. If we were working short-handed, we rounded-up and drove the cattle to a corral where we branded, marked and castrated. If we had plenty of help, we rounded-up and branded on the open range. This method was faster than when we had to pen the cattle. Once we had twenty hands at work, and held an open round-up about five miles southwest of the present site of Lubbock. We had two fires and two expert ropers. According to our tally sheets, in four hours we branded seven hundred and twenty calves.

Occasionally we got an old wild, outlaw steer in a round-up. He would be restless, and watch for a chance to make a get-away. He would keep the whole herd nervous, and at the first opportunity he would make a break for the open. A puncher would probably run a horse down getting him back. In the earlier days we had tried various schemes with these old outlaws; we would hobble them, and "side-line" them, but this was lots of trouble and was unsatisfactory. Finally someone discovered the system of "kneeing" these wild ones. The old outlaw would be roped and tied down. Then with a knife a puncher

would split the hide about an inch and a half between
the knee and ankle on one foreleg, and cut a small
leader or tendon. When the old steer was turned
loose he found his running days were over. He could
walk, or trot with a limp, but could not run. After
that, when he was in a herd, he wanted to remain.
This operation did not seem to hurt the animal. In
fact, it had the opposite effect; when he got so he
couldn't run his flesh off any more, he usually got
fat and could be shipped to market.

The I O A Company had leased the Dixie Pasture,
which lay in Lynn County, just south of our Middle
Pasture. It had been fenced by Major Johnson and
contained about 50,000 acres. Major Johnson lived
on the place and kept a postoffice called Percheon at
his house; but he never stocked the pasture. Part of
the time he leased it to the I O A Company, and
part of the time to other outfits. To the north of our
East Pasture we had 50,000 acres of open range
leased. In all, including our own range, we had over
a third of a million acres to work. We usually started
in the East Pasture, then worked the Middle Pasture,
then the Dixie Pasture, and next the West Pasture.
Then we rounded-up for the nesters on the west and
north, and held one round-up on leased open range
to the north of our East Pasture. Our calf crop usually ran from 4,000 to 7,000. The largest number we
ever branded in a single season was 7,500.

While working on the Plains we frequently
camped where there was no brush, nor anything to
stake our night horses to. We would dig a hole in

the ground four or five inches in diameter and eight
or ten inches deep. At the bottom of the hole we
would excavate to one side for about six inches. Then
we would make on that side a little trench just the
width of a lariat. We would tie a large knot in the
end of the rope, and place it in the enlarged excavation at the bottom, and bring the rope out through
the trench. Then we would fill the main hole and
tramp the dirt with our boot heels. If the ground
were not too wet, this system of staking was as good
as a bush or a stump.

In connection with round-ups we had the matter
of spaying. We did not spay all the heifers, but only
those we expected to use as beeves at the age of
three or four. Spaying was a much more delicate
operation than castration and required special treatment. The operation had to be done by a person of
skill and training. The male calves were castrated at
the time they were branded, and there was no particular risk unless screw worms got started. But the
female calves had to be held and driven to headquarters, where special equipment and a pasture were
provided. There were two methods of spaying. The
old way was to pull the heifer up by the heels with
a block and tackle attached to a heavy cross-beam
supported by two tall posts. An incision about four
inches long was made, and the "doc" ran his fingers
in and removed the ovaries. The incision was sewed
up and the animal was then driven into another corral
so that she would not have to be choused around
any more. After that it was better to keep the heifers

in a separate pasture for a few weeks until the wounds healed.

A newer method was to drive the heifer into a shoot, fasten her securely and make an incision in the side. The incision was smaller, and was made in the side just in front of the hip bone. This method seemed more humane in that it did not require stringing the animal up by the heels.

In November, 1889, I drove my first Cross C beef herd to Amarillo. We intended to start on November 4, but a heavy snow the night before caused me to postpone the drive. By November 11 the snow had melted enough for us to start. There were eight punchers in the crew besides myself and a negro cook and a negro wrangler. We left the Dixie Pasture with eighteen hundred steers, and camped the first night at the west mill in the Middle Pasture. On the twelfth we camped three miles north of the north mill in the Middle Pasture. On the thirteenth we got to Julian Lake about five miles northwest of Estacado. We laid over there a half day to let the cattle graze. On the fourteenth we drove the herd through the public square at Plainview, which at the time contained one store, one blacksmith shop, one three-room hotel, and a half dozen small, boxed residences. That night a fresh norther came up, and it began to snow again.

I lost one of my spurs during the night, and next morning it was not to be found. We had camped near the house of a Mr. Pepper, and I told him about losing the spur. A few months later Mr. Pepper was gathering cow-chips for fuel on the bed ground we used that night, and found my spur underneath a large chip. He returned it to me the next fall.

The next morning we threw the herd on the trail and faced snow and sleet all day. By the time we got to North Tule Canyon that night the snow was six inches deep. When we got the cattle bedded down, they gave us no more trouble, but we nearly froze. Our wood supply was getting low and the cowchips were covered with snow; so we hoarded our fuel for cooking purposes. The next day we passed Tulia. The town had just started, and there were two houses there. That night we camped half way between Tulia and Happy. After supper one of the boys told us how Happy got its name. It seems that a few years before some cowboys came unaware upon a family camped near the place. The people were singing, and were in an exuberant mood. The punchers went their way and called the place Happy Draugh. The weather had not abated any and the cattle could find very little to eat. The negroes were standing the cold badly. It seems that a negro can't stand the cold like a white man. All of us got our feet and ears frost-bitten. The next night we camped on the Frying Pan Ranch five miles south of Amarillo. On the evening of the tenth day we reached the stock-pens at Amarillo—only to find it would be several days before we could get cars to ship the steers to Chicago.

The cattle were hungry and lank as they had not had a good fill in several days, and now the prospect of having to hold them for another week on ground that had been nipped clean by other herds during the summer before, made the situation look bad. Next day I ran across the manager of the L X Ranch in a hotel in Amarillo and told him my troubles. He told me to put the herd in the L X pasture which was not over three miles north of the stock-pens. The water and grass there were good, and as the snow had melted, the herd got well filled again. This caused the cattle to bring several hundred dollars more when they reached Chicago. When we got home I wrote the vice-president of the company, Mr. Wheelock, that I would never again drive a herd to Amarillo later than October.

During the seven years I was manager of the I O A Ranch we drove twenty herds to Amarillo. Ordinarily, we drove in September and October. There was usually little or no surface water at that time of the year, and living watering places were far between. We would gather a herd and drive it to Yellow House Creek just east of where Lubbock now stands, and hold the cattle on the creek until about two o'clock in the afternoon. Then we would start north and drive all night. By midnight the cattle would begin to get thirsty, and fifteen miles before we could get to Running Water they could smell the water. Then they would begin to trot and try to run. I would have to put a majority of the hands in front to hold the cattle back. About daylight we would reach Running Water, a distance of fifty miles. Here we camped to give the cattle time to rest and get full of grass and water. I drove the first night for two reasons. The first night on the trail, cattle are restless and mill around most of the time, so I thought that if they were walking about, they might as well be applying that energy on getting to our destination; and the long dry lap to Running Water could best be made at night.

Our next move depended upon how dry the weather had been. If it had been unusually dry, we would not expect to find water on the Middle Tule and would have to make the Tierra Blanca near Canyon City. In that case, we laid over at Running Water for a day and night, and started the next afternoon. It would take all night and until the next afternoon to make the sixty-five miles to Tierra Blanca. This lap was hard on the men, horses and cattle. We were all mighty tired and lank when we got to Canyon. We camped there and made the short drive to Amarillo next day. When we found water in the Middle Tule the trip was not nearly so hard on us.

After the railroad got there in 1887, Amarillo became the biggest shipping point in Texas for a number of years. Cattle were driven to Amarillo from Brewster, Pecos and Valverde Counties. Drovers watered on the head of the Middle Concho, the Colorado, Tobacco Creek in Dawson County, the Yellow House near where the cemetery at Lubbock is now located, and followed our route on to Amarillo. The trail came through the Middle Pasture of the I O A Ranch. I had a man who devoted all his time during the driving season to conducting trail herds across our range. He met the herds at the south

gate, went with the outfit to see that none of our
cattle got mixed with the trail herd, stood by while
the cattle watered at the creek, and saw the herd out
through the north gate. It usually took about a day
to get a herd through our range.

In the summer of 1889 a herd came by from
South Texas. The outfit was bossed by a man by the
name of B——, a big, muscular fellow with a heavy,
drooping, black mustache. He wore one of the biggest
guns I ever saw. B—— wanted to camp inside the
pasture on the creek. Our man told him he could.
That night his outfit killed an I O A calf for beef;
and next morning before our man got there, B——
tore down three panels of our north fence and drove
through. He tore the fence down rather than go a
little farther west to the gate. When our man came in
and reported the matter, I was furious. I rode pell-
mell to Estacado and swore out a warrant against
B——, and went with Deputy Sheriff Sandefer to
serve it. Sandefer had a reputation as a daring man;
he later died with his boots on in a duel with another
one of his kind. When we overtook B——, and told
him he was under arrest and would have to go with
us to Estacado, he gave us one hard look as if he
were deciding whether to comply or whether he
would shoot us, and then smiled and said, "All
right." When we got to Estacado, we compromised
by his paying for the damage done the fence and
$25 for the calf. The affair delayed his herd for a
day. I would never have said anything about the
calf if he had not torn the fence down. Sometime

later I learned that B—— was a bad "hombre" down on the border. He had a couple of notches on his gun for white men, and he had gotten several Mexicans, but he didn't count notches for them. The next year he came through with another herd and again camped on the creek. He rode down to headquarters to see me. He came up laughing and asked if I remembered him. I told him most truthfully that I certainly did. I might have added that I had thought of him many times since I discovered who he was. That time he didn't kill an I O A calf or tear down any fence. If he had, I am not sure I would have done anything about it.

In 1893 we were driving a herd of steers to Amarillo. There had been a severe drouth for several months, and the ground was dry, cracked, and parched. One afternoon when we were west of Tulia a rain cloud came up. It poured for two hours. When it began to let up we noticed the ground was literally covered with little frogs about the size of the end of a lead pencil. The cloud was a local one, and we moved out of its range in three or four miles. The frogs extended as far as the rain did. That night the boys had a big argument about where the frogs came from. It seemed to be the consensus of opinion that the frogs had rained down from the cloud. I told them that if that were the case there would have been frogs in the pockets of our slickers, but the boys were not convinced.

The matter of neighboring outfits killing each other's yearlings for beef was almost a common practice. The T Anchor people on the Tierra Blanca always had a wagon down in this region during the summer gathering strays at the round-ups. The wagon oufit often killed an I O A calf for meat. We did not have much chance to retaliate because our cattle seldom ever drifted north. In 1890 I was driving a trail herd through the T Anchor range, and we beefed a fat T Anchor cow. When we got to Amarillo I saw the manager, John Hutson, and told him what we had done. He said, "Ah, that's all right, let's go and get a drink."

From February to April each year we had to "ride bogs." There were boggy places all along Yellow House Creek from Singer's Store to the east line of East Pasture, but the worst ones were northeast of the present site of Lubbock. Cattle got thin during the winter, and by February the weakest ones did not have enough strength left to extricate themselves from the bogs. Four men rode the creek in pairs. When they found a cow bogged, they put a rope on her horns and pulled her out by the saddle horn. If it were a calf, they placed the rope around its neck. Once we found an old cow mired so deep that one horse could not pull her out. We placed another rope on her and pulled at her with two horses. When we got her out and removed the ropes, we found we had torn her horns and the top part of her skull loose from her head. She walked off with her horns flopping like a mule's ears. When we shipped her to market next fall, she was slick and fat, but her horns were still flopping. After our experience with her, however, when we had to use a second rope on an animal, we placed it around the neck. During the seven years we pulled several thousand cattle out of the bogs and never killed one.

Ranchmen lost cattle every year. A dry year would cause grass to be short, and the cattle would start the winter in poor condition. With a mild winter there would be losses, but a blizzard would take hundreds or, perhaps, thousands. Yearly losses ran from five to twenty per cent and averaged about ten per cent. Some ranches undertook to skin the animals that died. It was customary to give men half the hides to do the skinning. Two men usually worked together. If the skinners were honest, the business could be conducted with some profit to the ranch. But if the skinners were dishonest, the ranch would be better off to let the hides rot on the carcasses. An unprincipled skinner would not help up weak animals, as he was supposed to do. He would drive cattle into bogs and let them die. Some skinners resorted to killing cattle for their hides. Their method was to drive a nail behind the horns into the brain of the animal. This left no sign, and no one would suspect that the animal had been killed, as the head was not skinned. After a year or two, however, when the hide had slipped from the skull, the nail showed plainly. The I O A Ranch was one of the ranches that did undertake to skin its dead cattle, but we never let skinning contracts to anyone that we did not have absolute trust in.

Prairie fires were a source of worry to ranch managers. Destruction of the grass upon which cattle subsisted was next to the destruction of the cattle themselves. There was danger of fires during more than half the year. In a year of average rainfall, grass put out in April, grew during May and probably June, became dry and brown during July and August, was green again after the fall rains in September and October, was killed by frost in November, and remained dry and crisp until April. For two or three months in the summer, and for four or five months in the winter, grass was in a condition to be destroyed by fire. During these periods all hands on the ranch kept a sharp lookout for grass smoke. A tiny thread of smoke on any part of the range would have half a hundred pair of eyes on various ranches watching it. If it increased in volume and showed the unmistakable evidences of burning grass, it was a signal for all hands to drop what they were doing and start to the fire with all speed possible.

The first man to reach the fire killed the nearest cow. Custom provided that no matter whose brand was on the animal, she must be sacrificed to the fire. They would remove the head and split the carcass into halves, leaving the hide on; this would make two drags. One man would tie his lariat to a forefoot and another man would tie his lariat to a hind foot of a drag and, pulling it between them, would ride along the line of fire. Two other men would take the other drag and go in the opposite direction. They rode in a gallop, and when their horses began to fag, other riders relieved them. The drags would blot

out most of the fire, and other men following on foot
with gunny sacks or with their slickers would beat
out the remaining fragments. In this way, with sufficient help we could put out fifteen or twenty miles
of fire within a few hours, provided the wind was
not too high.

We kept fire guards plowed around the I O A
Ranch, and seldom had a fire within the pasture.
But each year there were two or three north or west
of us. We always turned out to help fight these fires
lest they get to our lines and jump our fire guards.

The two chief causes for fires are lightning and
carelessness of punchers in dropping their matches
after lighting a cigarette. Occasionally a fire would
get started, however, when there was not a cloud in
sight nor a human being within ten miles. This has
puzzled many a plainsman. I was riding alone one
day, and there were no clouds in view. All at once I
noticed a small blaze in the grass about a hundred
yards in front of me. I started toward the fire in a
run, and a flock of curlews flew up near the fire. The
grass was short and there was no breeze; so I had
little trouble in getting the fire put out. Then I began
to look for a cause. I found three or four charred
matches. I concluded that they had been accidently
dropped there by some one, and the curlews had ig-
nited one of them by pecking it. Since then I have
been quite sure that birds are instrumental in starting
some fires.

Another source of anxiety to the cattleman was
the lobo wolf. The ranchman dreaded lobos more

than he did prairie fires. One lobo would do more harm than a dozen coyotes. Coyotes were death on sheep, and at unguarded moments might happen on a calf not old enough to take care of itself. They seemed to concentrate their ravages on the sheep interests, but the lobo apparently had the same disdain for sheep that the cowboy had for the sheepherder. The lobo's palate craved beef, and he resorted to mutton only when beef was not to be had.

Nothing was more exasperating to a cowman than to be riding across the range and come upon the partially devoured carcass of a fine, fat yearling. A grown lobo, or "loafer," in a cattle country, would likely kill from ten to twenty head of cattle a year. When there were as many as two along they often killed cows for the sake of eating their unborn calves. A female lobo, with a den of cubs to support, always had a ravenous appetite. She preferred a fat calf, but in the absence of tenderer meat, she would tackle the toughest cow in the pasture. The average ranch probably sustained more damage from lobos than from cattle thieves.

The brakes below the Caprock had many splendid breeding places for lobos, and the arroyos which drained into Yellow House Canyon were equally as good. There was a ridge about two miles southwest of the I O A headquarters we called "Loafer Ridge." An old bitch made her den in the same hole every year. We got a litter of pups from it each year for three years before we caught the old wolf.

The lobos got so busy in 1892 that for six months

I employed two men who devoted all their time to hunting. I furnished them grub, horses and horse feed and gave them $20 a scalp. Lobos are so smart it is practically useless to try to trap for them. The only effective way of getting a lobo during the 90's was to jump and run him down with hounds and horses. The two men killed twenty-five during the winter.

About a year later I left the I O A headquarters one morning on a slow, easy-gaited horse. I came out of the canyon some distance east of where the Lubbock cemetery is and saw a lobo devouring a calf in the open, south of the canyon. When the lobo saw me, he started south in a long run. I took after him but my horse was so slow I could barely keep in sight. I figured that he would eventually turn back towards the canyon. He gained about two miles on me, and finally began to veer to the east. Then I began to swing inside the circle to save my horse. As he circled, we got closer together. Finally, I got close enough to perceive the wolf was losing speed and his tongue was hanging out. By that time we were running parallel, due east about a hundred yards apart. He was so tired that my slow horse could keep up. I knew it would only be a matter of time until he would try to break past me and get to the canyon; so I decided to try my hand at roping him when he made his break. Suddenly he turned toward me in a desperate effort to get to the canyon. My lariat swung true and he was soon dangling at the end of the rope. I was so proud of my feat that

I drug him all the way to headquarters as tangible evidence to substantiate my story. Had he not been gorged on veal, he probably would have made his escape, but the day was too hot and dusty and the run too long for him to carry the ten or fifteen pounds of beef and make his get-away.

CHAPTER XIII

YARNS

ONE evening in the early fall of 1891, while on a round-up in the West Pasture, we got through supper early and had an hour or two to sit around the fire before we crawled into our "hot-rolls." One of the first northers of the season had blown up the day before, and the air was so crisp that evening that the fire felt good. The boys kept adding cow chips, and the coals glowed red but never blazed much. Some of the punchers sprawled full length on the ground, some leaned back against their saddles, and some sat on their heels and smoked cigarettes.

We got to talking about mirages. To cow-punchers who knew nothing of scientific explanations, there was something mysterious about mirages. All the boys who had been on the Plains very long had seen freakish things happen. I had observed cattle which looked twenty-five feet tall, grazing near a mirage, and a man riding a horse that appeared forty feet tall. All kinds of peculiar things have happened in a mirage. Men have traveled miles towards a most realistic lake only to find it was not there. At a time

171

when there were no houses, fences or trees within forty miles, one frequently saw such things only a few miles away. New-comers on the Plains, unaccustomed to the peculiarities of mirages, sometimes thought of them as good or bad omens.

I told the boys about a mirage I saw during the spring of 1890. Estacado was twenty-two miles from the I O A headquarters and over a considerable ridge. The region immediately around Estacado was much more rolling than land commonly is in the vicinity of Crosby County. Approaching from the south, one could not see the town until he was in four or five miles of the place. One clear, frosty morning I stepped out into the back yard and saw Estacado elevated just above the horizon. Every house was visible. I could have counted the panes in the windows in the west and south sides of the courthouse. I could see horses tied to the hitching posts in front of the stores and blacksmith shop, and people walking about the place. It seemed to me that, with the aid of field glasses, I would have been able to recognize the faces of the individuals.

In the late fall of 1890 I witnessed another illusion equally strange. Our rounding-up outfit was camped about eight miles from the Yellow House Canyon, practically due south of Buffalo Springs. The morning was chilly, still and frosty. When I got up between daylight and sunrise, the cook called to me, "Boss, I thought we camped several miles from the Canyon last night."

"We did."

"Look, we are right on the edge of it this morning."

I looked, and I never beheld a more perfect mirage. It was so realistic it would have fooled an old-timer. There was the bottom of the Canyon just below us, water running along the creek, a few hackberry trees along the edges of the water course, and cattle grazing along the sides of the Canyon. I saw familiar landmarks in the creek, trees and rocks. It seemed that I could have thrown a rock into the center of the Canyon. If I had not known that we were eight miles from the rim of the Canyon and over a slight rise, I would have sworn we were on the very edge.

"Last spring," said T Bar Dick, "while I was 'reping' for our outfit over on the Syndicate range, I heard an old puncher tell about a mirage he had seen about fourteen years before when he was a buffalo hunter. His camp was beside a lake in one of the wide, shallow basins on the Plains. He got lost from camp and rode several days looking for it. There was plenty of water in the lakes and buffaloes everywhere; so he was in no danger in that respect, but he had to get back to camp eventually. Each morning he would get his bearings the best he could when the sun came up, and ride all day eyeing the horizon in every direction for the lost camp. One morning after riding a couple of hours, he looked back and saw an unusual mirage behind him. There were buffaloes, wild horses, antelope, and wolves moving about without touching the earth. The reality of the scene impressed him so much he stopped to study it awhile. Directly he recognized his camp beside the lake. There were his wagon, piles of buffalo hides, and his horses grazing not far away. He knew enough about mirages to know that this was a reflected image of his camp. He took his bearing and headed back toward the mirage. The illusion soon vanished, but he kept the direction. He rode hard all day, and just before sun-down he topped a ridge, and there was his camp. That morning when he saw the mirage he must have been thirty or forty miles away."

None of us who had been on the Plains for a season or more doubted the truth of this story. "Shorty" Anderson had been stretched by the fire listening with rapt attention. Shorty always had a mischievous twinkle in his eye, and when he was up to something the twinkle became downright devilish.

"Speaking of buffaloes," he said, "I was out on the Plains once before any cowmen had ever ventured on top of the Caprock. I don't suppose there was a tree, or a post, or a man in fifty miles. I rode up on a ridge once and saw a big buffalo bull grazing near a lake. He didn't see me, and I rode back quickly and circled around to get on the wind side. I had only my Colt 45, and my horse was afraid of buffaloes. I thought my only chance was to leave my horse over the ridge and stalk the bull on foot. I figured that if everything worked just right I stood a chance to get within pistol range. I got up within thirty yards before the big brute sighted me. He looked at me a

moment and couldn't decide whether to run at me or
from me. In either case, I decided I had better let
him have it. I banged away at him, and didn't hit
where I aimed. The first shot caused him to turn
towards me. I let him have five more, but you can't
kill a buffalo with a 45 unless you hit right behind
his shoulder blade. If he had been in doubt about
what to do beforehand, he didn't have any doubts
after I put six lumps of lead under his hide. He gave
a wild bellow and took after me. My horse was a
mile away, and somehow I didn't get started in that
direction. The bull gained on me for a little bit; he
was snorting and blowing and it seemed like I could
feel his breath. But after the first hundred yards I
began to hold my own."

Shorty stopped suddenly as if that was the end of
the story, but "Red" Wheeler couldn't leave him in
that predicament.

"What did you do next," asked Red.

"I climbed a tree."

"But you said there was not a tree in fifty miles."

"Well, you see, it was this away. It happened that
one of those mirages like the boss has been telling
about was right in front of me. There was a big
hackberry tree growing by a water hole. Well, I
climbed that mirage tree."

The boys bellowed, swayed, and slapped their
knees. Most of them concluded that the joke was
on Red, but one or two took a sheepish side glance
at me. I was never any hand at repartee, and was
for letting it pass. But there was a young puncher

there from Estacado. He was about five feet eight
inches tall, slender, wiry, hot tempered and could
ride any horse in the country. He was easy to get
along with until you nettled him, and then it was too
bad. The biggest, toughest rough-neck in the outfit
would have thought twice before getting this stripling
riled up. He had an Irish wit and a deep booming
voice like all United States senators aspire to have.
The boys were mighty leery about pulling anything
on him. His name was Winford Hunt. When the
haw-hawing died down, Winford came to my and
Red's rescue.

"Now, Shorty, don't you reckon that buffalo bull
that was chasing you was just a mirage buffalo?"

Then it was Shorty's turn for the back-slapping.

This caused the conversation to leave the question
of mirages, and become general. George Boles told a
story that I never have been quite sure whether it
was truth or fiction.

"There was a puncher named Tom Collier who
used to work on the Square and Compass back in '85
when Rollie here was manager down there. Tom was
about eighteen when he came out to start punching.
He had run away from home on account of his step-
mother. He had several smaller brothers and sisters
whom he thought a great deal of. In the fall, he decided to pay them a visit. He went back to his home
near Austin, and the folks gave him a big welcome.
Even his step-mother seemed glad to see him. He
entertained his family and the neighbors awhile
showing how well he could ride a horse and throw a

rope. In a few days, he heard there was to be a circus
in Austin. He had saved his wages, so he decided to
give all his brothers and sisters a treat. None of them
had ever been to town before, and they were all excited about it. They loaded into the farm wagon and
drove to Austin. Out in the edge of town they came
to a blacksmith shop that was all posted over with
pictures advertising the circus. There were clowns,
trapeze actors doing stunts, animals with the trainers,
and scenes from the parade. The posters announced
in box-car letters when and where the show was to
be, but neither Tom nor any of his brothers or
sisters could read. When they saw the pictures they
concluded that this must be the circus. So Tom went
in and asked the blacksmith if they could look at
the show. The blacksmith said certainly, to go ahead
and look all they wanted to. Tom led the kids
around and they looked at the pictures a long time.
Then Tom offered to pay the blacksmith, but the
smith wouldn't take any pay. They got in the wagon
and went home, thinking they had seen the circus.
Afterwards, Tom found out his mistake, and when
he came back to the Square and Compass next spring,
he told me about it."

Pete McSpadden had not said a word as yet. He
had worked for the Llanos in the early 80's, but was
now "reping" for the Slaughter outfit. Pete was a
versatile fellow, a top hand; he could make a political
speech, preach, and even pray on occasion. He was
one of the best story-tellers on the range, and when

he began to sit up, we knew he was keyed up to tell one.

"I was just thinking about a cyclone we had back in '81. I was working for the Llanos, and we had a puncher in the outfit by the name of Sam Golden. Sam was one of the best hands I ever saw. He would do anything on a ranch from cooking sour-dough and building corrals to acting as top-rope man at the round-ups. He was born in Tennessee, but was raised near Uvalde, Texas. He joined our outfit in 1880, a tall, rough, handsome fellow with a pair of sharp, clear eyes that bespoke veracity.

"We had just rounded-up a big bunch of cattle about where Post City is now located. There were about twenty hands with the outfit, and we were working hard, for a cloud was gathering back on the Plains to the northwest, and we wanted to get the branding done before the cloud-bank came up. The cattle became more and more restless. They seemed to sense something in the air. Before we even got the irons hot, we saw it was useless to start branding. The cattle were milling and bawling and ready to stampede at the drop of a hat. The cloud was getting a move on. Lightning was doing zig-zags just beyond the rim of the Caprock, and thunder was making a continuous roll. The boss hollered to all the boys to get their slickers on and to get ready to hold the herd. By the time we did that, the cloud was sweeping down off the Caprock. The cattle were sniffing the wind and showing the whites of their eyes. We knew they were all set for a stampede. Most of the

boys were on the east side of the herd so as to hold
the critters as long as they could, and then if the
cattle did stampede, the boys would be in front so
they could eventually turn the herd.

"About the time the cloud came off the Caprock,
we noticed a small funnel-shaped cloud moving just
in front. It was coming straight at us, and the tail
was swooping down and touching the ground every
once and awhile. It hit our chuck wagon and took
it up in the air. About that time the cattle broke, and
we didn't have time to watch the cyclone any more.
When the herd started, Sam Golden was on the west
side of the cattle. He rode like fury behind the herd
for a half mile, and then the cyclone picked him and
his horse up, carried them over in front of the herd
and set them down as gently as could be. While up in
the air, however, Sam had lost his hat and his quirt.
He helped turn the herd in about three miles and got
the cattle to milling. In thirty minutes the storm was
over, and the boys started back with the cattle. When
they got to the place where Sam had lost his hat, he
looked up and saw it about a hundred yards in the air
slowly settling to earth. He maneuvered his horse
around so that the hat came down on his head with
the point in front.

"Sam kept looking up for his quirt. How it had
gotten away was a mystery. He had it fastened to the
horn of his saddle with a leather string, and the quirt,
string, and all had disappeared. But Sam looked in
vain for the quirt, for it didn't come down. I worked
with Sam in the vicinity several times after that, and

every time he passed that spot, he would stop and look up. He was still expecting his quirt to come down."

Uncle Tang Martin, who was "reping" for the X I T people, took a long-range shot at the fire with a squirt of tobacco juice, and said, "Well, I've never had much close-up experience with cyclones, but when I was a boy back in Alabama, I was a great athlete. I wasn't so good at running, but I was a champion when it came to jumping. I believe I still hold a world's record for the standing jump."

"How far could you jump, Uncle Tang?" asked Shorty.

"Fifty-six feet."

Shorty whistled, and the rest of us wanted to whistle. Uncle Tang let it soak for about a minute, and then he went on, "Well, you see, my pa was after me with a hay-rake. I jumped one foot, and landed in a well fifty-five feet deep."

When the air cleared, Uncle Tang told us some more about the athletic traits of his family.

"My pa was a strong man. I dare say he was the stoutest person in the state. They were having a contest at a county fair once to see how much the various contestants could carry on their backs. They were carrying buckshot. Pa had seven bushels on his back, and told them to put on some more. They kept piling more and more shot on pa's back until he bogged down knee deep through the rock pavement."

Everyone was quiet for a few minutes, and then Winford Hunt said, "I had a ghost experience about two years ago, but I hesitate to tell about it now after these wild cyclone and jumping yarns."

"Ah, go ahead, kid, it don't make any difference whether it's so or not," said Uncle Tang.

"It's so, anyway, whether you believe it or not. After all, it doesn't matter, I suppose, who believes it. I want to say in the beginning that I am not a person to have presentiments. I have a sister who takes stock in such things, but none of that for me.

"It was in November, 1889. I was just an overgrown boy in the Quaker colony at Estacado. My father was the only physician in three or four counties and was away from home most of the time making long distance medical calls. We had about a hundred head of cattle, and it was my business to look after the stock. There were no fences, and cold rains caused the cattle to drift away. We had just had three days of continuous rains. The ground was soaked so badly a horse would sink almost to his fetlocks walking across the prairie. On the fourth day the rain stopped, but a misty fog hung over the ground. You couldn't see a cow over a quarter of a mile.

"I wanted to start out to find the cattle. There was danger of a hard freeze, and a blizzard would have caused the cattle to drift to kingdom come. Mother did not want me to start; she was afraid I would get lost on the prairie. My older brother thought I ought to go, so together we convinced mother, and I saddled my pony and started. My horse's name was Richard Coeur de Lion, but I called him Dick for short. I suppose that must indicate the kind of literature I was reading then. Dick was a great pony; I could catch him anywhere. He would come to me as far as he could hear me call, and he was the best cow pony in the colony. He could turn on a dime, and all you had to do was to show him which cow you wanted. Dick and I had been doing the reping for the colony at neighboring round-ups for a couple of years. I had told mother that morning that you couldn't lose Dick, and that was the winning argument.

"We were gone all day. Along in the morning it had started raining again, and we got soaked. In the late afternoon the clouds lifted a little, and looked as if they might drift over. I was cold, hungry, and disappointed, for I had not found the cattle. So I started home. It was not long before the clouds began to thicken again, and it began to lighten and thunder.

"There was an old bachelor who lived about five miles from Estacado. His name was John White. He had some cattle, four sections of land fenced, and lived in a dugout. His dugout was made in the conventional way. A hole was excavated about four feet deep. The walls were built up about three feet with sod. A ridge-pole was placed across the center, and smaller poles cross-ways. On these were placed brush, a layer of sod, and then a layer of earth.

"I struck John White's east fence and turned south, for I knew that would take me directly towards home. It was just getting dusk when I got to John's dugout. The clouds had settled down, and I couldn't see anything except when it lightened. I

noticed that John's cows were bawling as if they had
not been fed. As I neared the place Dick began to
prance, and act as if he were greatly agitated about
something. He seldom acted that way, and I knew he
wasn't just putting on, for he had been going hard
all day and was dog tired. By the time we got opposite the dugout, Dick was rearing up and snorting.
I was trying to quiet him when a big flash of lightning came, and I saw John White standing by the
windmill not twenty yards away. I hollered at him
and waved my hand. Dick shied and started to run.
I had to give him all my attention for a moment.
We were about seventy-five yards down the fence
when the next flash came. Again I saw John White
standing about twenty yards slightly to one side, this
time on the opposite side of the fence. I was sure it
was he, and hollered and waved my hand again. Dick
shied and made tracks. As we hurried on I kept wondering how John could have gotten the seventy-five
yards or more and crossed over the fence as quickly
as we did, when Dick was running.

"I got home about an hour later, and then had
nine cows to feed and milk. It was nine o'clock before
I got in for supper. Mother had the food hot, and
we were sitting in the old kitchen a little later when
there was a sharp knock at the door. Mother opened
it, and a neighbor of John White's rushed in. He
was frightened, and blear-eyed. He had gone to
John's dugout a short time after I had passed and
found John dead. The neighbor had then come pell-
mell for father. Father was away at the time, but

came in within an hour and started immediately to
John's place.

"The rain had caused the roof to cave in on John
while he was asleep the night before. The ridge-
pole had struck him over the heart and caved his
chest in. The rain had washed dirt down all over
him except his face. That was washed clean and
had a pale, ghostly look. Father estimated that he
had been dead fifteen or eighteen hours when I
passed the place at dusk.

"The strange part of it all was the fact I didn't
know he was dead until sometime after I had seen his
ghost twice. I had never dreamed of his being dead,
and at the time I was as sure I saw him as I am sure
I am living right now."

This story, having a ring of reality to it, and
dealing with ghosts and death, caused the punchers
to quiet down. No one felt in the mood to tell another, and soon the boys began to slip off one at a time
and crawl into their "hot-rolls".

CHAPTER XIV

CLOSING OUT THE I O A RANCH

ONE Sunday soon after we came to the I O A Ranch in 1888, I took my wife and children to Estacado to church. The Quaker Colony had been established there in 1878 by Paris Cox. It took us two hours to drive the twenty-two miles in a two-horse buckboard. The drive reminded me of the time I had first encountered the Quakers in 1881. While working for the "22" outfit, two other punchers and I were riding up the bed of Salt Fork near the Caprock one day when we heard singing. We rounded a turn in the river and saw about a dozen women and children gathering wild plums. They were singing religious hymns; and so intent were they on their singing and plum-gathering, they did not see us until were were within fifty yards of them. When one of them saw us, she screamed, and then they all screamed and scattered among the bushes like quail. We rode on by without trying to round any of them up; and then we got to wondering why they acted so scary. One of the punchers 'lowed that they must have thought we were Indians. When we came to think it out we did look pretty wild. We had not shaved or had our hair cut for months, and had been living in a dugout besides.

But to return to 1888, when we got to Estacado, we found practically the entire community assembled in the Quaker Church. The house was built of boxing plank and was about sixteen by twenty feet. The benches were crude and made of plank. A big box stove in the middle of the room burned wood and cowchips. The wood had to be hauled from Blanco Canyon or the breaks below the Caprock. When we went in, the Quakers were sitting around with their hats on, not saying anything. Most of them seemed to be in a deep, brown study, but some of the less devout interrupted their spiritual meditations long enough to look us over. I supposed they were just waiting for the preacher to come, or something. In a few moments, without any announcement, someone started a song and the others joined in. When the song was over they all hushed again, and I thought the preacher would surely be along pretty soon. In a few minutes some old gentleman without warning started praying. He prayed awhile and stopped, and everything got quiet again. Then somebody else started a song. After that, all was quiet for awhile, and then one of the older men got up abruptly and read from the Bible, and commented for a minute or two on what he had read. When he got up, I thought he was the preacher, but when he sat down we didn't seem to be any farther along than before. Except for a cough and someone's scraping his feet on the floor there was not a sound for five minutes, when a woman started a song in a rather high, shaky voice. Another quiet spell, Scripture reading, quiet, prayer, quiet, Scripture reading, quiet, song, quiet, and then someone announced the service was over. I kept looking for the preacher to turn up until the very last, but afterwards found out they didn't have a preacher in the sense that most Protestant churches do.

After the service the Quakers were very friendly with us, and one family urged us to go home with them for dinner. We went and found that Quakers lived pretty well—fried chicken, gravy, biscuits, ham, wild plum preserves, and fried pies. We learned that the Quakers had come to the Plains ten years before with high hopes, but as the years passed, they had become more and more discouraged. Attempting to farm so far from a railroad was slow going. They raised good crops, but to market anything except a small part of what they raised was out of the question.

During the next few years we had many pleasant contacts with the Quakers. A lot of people thought they were queer, and wouldn't have anything to do with them; but that was because they never did get acquainted. All the Quakers I knew were splendid citizens. After the colony broke up a few years later, some of them went back to Illinois and Indiana, and others scattered on the Plains and became Methodists.

In 1889 the directors of the I O A Ranch decided to try farming in connection with the ranch. The vice-president wrote, asking me what I thought of raising five hundred to a thousand acres of sorghum to feed steers during the winter so as to have them fat in the spring and sell at high prices. I replied that I did not think it was practical, but the directors were disposed to have a sorghum field put in, anyway. They placed Frank Wheelock in charge of the farming operations. He broke two hundred and fifty acres south of the Canyon and broadcast the sorghum field. He sowed three bushels to the acre and the seed cost two dollars and a half a bushel. The seed alone amounted to $7.50 an acre as the initial expense. The sorghum grew very well, and Wheelock cut it with a mowing machine. But the experiment was too costly to be practical. The company tried raising sorghum one more year, and then gave it up as a failure.

I was interested in knowing whether or not cotton would grow on the Plains. When I came to the I O A Ranch in December, 1888, I found some cotton seed which the manager before me had hauled from Colorado City to feed to his milch cow. I put enough of the seed aside to plant a patch in the spring. In May, 1889, I planted three acres. I did not cultivate or thin the plants in anyway. Neither did I gather the cotton, but I judged the patch made over a half bale to the acre. I predicted then that some day the South Plains would be a great cotton country; but until a railroad was built cotton farming would not be practical.

In 1892 I unthoughtedly introduced crab-grass into Lubbock County. I bought some fruit trees from the Munson Nursery at Denison, and set them out at a place I was improving for myself about two miles north of the I O A headquarters. The trees had crab-grass around the roots. When I planted the trees I threw the grass out in the garden. In the spring it took root and began to spread. I was busy that year and paid little attention to the grass. It matured, and the seed was spread by the cattle. In a few years there was crab-grass all over the country.

We experimented from time to time in a small way with various kinds of foraging plants. In 1892 we tried meadow oat grass, but found it was not adaptable. We tried millet, rye and other winter crops, but with machinery dear, and the cost of farming operations high, we found that the only economical way to raise cattle during the 90's was on native grass.

Orchards were not practical, because freezes in the spring killed the fruit on an average of two years out of three, and the life cycle of fruit trees was short. A person was lucky if he got one or two fruit crops before the trees died. Often the fruit that a tree would yield would not pay the original cost of the tree.

In the summer of 1889 my wife was at headquarters alone with the children one day. She happened to look out of a window and saw a half dozen Indians coming down the Canyon from the west. They were the first Indians my wife had ever seen, but she had grown up hardby the frontier and had heard scores of stories about Indians. Her first thought when she saw these, riding down the trail bare-headed and in single file, was that they were bent on plunder and murder. She got the children in the house in a hurry and locked the door. Then she watched the Indians through the window. When her first alarm subsided, she began to notice that they did not act as if they were on a scalping expedition. Their horses were poor and jaded, and the Indians drew up like travelers do before a strange house when they want something. I rode in sight about that time, and the Indians saw me and waited. Two or three could speak broken English. It seemed that they belonged on a reservation in New Mexico and were going to visit some of their kinsmen on a reservation in Indian Territory. They had been through this country several times before and knew the landmarks. They wanted some sugar and coffee, which I gave them, and they trailed on down the Canyon. Two or three of this party, together with some others, came by the following summer, and again in 1891. The last party seemed pretty well discouraged by so much barbed wire being strung over the country. I suppose that was the reason they never came through again.

In the summer of 1890 we had some fence-cutting trouble. Several nesters with small herds of cattle were located north of the I O A range. They would not go to the expense of putting down wells and erecting windmills. They depended on the lakes until they dried up, and then they were up against it. The easiest thing to do was to cut stretches of our fence, and let their cattle come to Yellow House Creek or to our windmills. We knew pretty well who the fence-cutters were, but we were unable to catch them in the act. I wrote Governor Sayers about the trouble, and he authorized me to offer an executive reward for indictable information concerning the fence-cutters. When I let it be known that the governor was offering a reward, the trouble ceased.

Our relations with our other neighbors were more pleasant. To the south in Lynn County was the T Bar Ranch, owned by the Tahoka Cattle Company. Colonel W. C. Young was interested in it; J. T. Lofton was secretary, and C. O. Edwards was a principal stockholder. Later, Edwards came to own all the ranch.

To the southwest was the N U N Ranch. John Nunn had moved to Scurry County with a small herd of cattle during the late 70's. He kept the increase, and by 1885 he had fifteen or twenty thousand head. Then he moved to Terry County, and located a few miles southeast of where Meadow was later established. When cattle prices went down in 1885, 1886, and 1887, he held his cattle and started borrowing money. At the same time he was at a big expense getting his land watered. All the while the rustlers were working him heavy. By 1890 he was broke and his creditors took over his land and cattle. They kept the N U N brand until the ranch was settled up.

To the east, occupying the southwest corner of Crosby County, was the Three H, H H ⊥ Ranch, owned by the St. Louis Cattle Company. The headquarters was on Yellow House Creek, about seven miles from the west line of Crosby County. Most of

the stock was owned by Charles Schmieding of St.
Louis, and John T. Beal was manager.

The few differences we had with these ranches
were settled amicably by arbitration. Each party
would select an arbitrator and the two arbitrators
would select a third. The three made an award which
was always accepted. This means of judicature was
swift and inexpensive. It obliterated slow and costly
court proceedings. A cow could be dead with old age
before a court decision could usually be had, and the
expense would be greater than the value of the animal.

Occasionally our strays would get in a trail herd
being shipped to market. We frequently recovered
the money these strays sold for through the Northwest Texas Stock Raisers' Association. The Association kept inspectors at all the major market points
to watch for strays belonging to members of the
Association. For instance, in 1889, three of our steers
arrived in St. Louis with a Two Buckle shipment.
The association's inspector claimed the steers for
the I O A Company, and we received the money
through the Association. Membership in the Association cost the I O A Ranch about twenty-five dollars
a year, and some years the amount of cattle recovered
did not exceed that amount. The main value of the
Association, however, lay in prevention rather than
recovery. Had it not been in existence, the possibili-
ties for shipping other people's strays would have
been increased, and our losses much greater.

One day in the spring of 1891 I was riding on the

Plains and came to a bundle of snakes. It was about the size of a bushel measure, all coiling and writhing. After watching awhile, I observed there were two tails and one head. I could not understand it. I fired three shots into the bundle, and then got a stick and began to untwist the pile of snakes. I found that a large bull snake was trying to swallow a rattlesnake of equal size and had him about half down. After that I never killed a bull snake unless he was near my chicken house.

During the 80's and 90's we frequently saw a little animal on the Plains called a "swift". It was about the size of a maltese cat, though its body was a little longer. It belonged to the fox family and had a brownish color. It could outrun a jack rabbit. I have chased swifts on horses many times, but was able to run one down only once. On that occasion there were four of us cowboys all mounted on fresh horses. By taking shortcuts we finally got it. The ground was hard and dry, and its feet were torn and bleeding. Some of its toe nails were hanging loose. If the ground had been soft I am sure we would never have outrun it.

There were lots of antelope on the Plains as late as 1890. My twenty years of observation of antelope convinced me that the young are born practically at the same time each spring. I never saw an antelope fawn before May 1 and I never saw one newly born after May 10. It seemed that all the borning took place within a week or so.

A tame antelope exhibits some of the same tem-

peramental characteristics that a goat does. I caught
a fawn once and took it to headquarters on the I O A
Ranch as a pet for the children. It made an interesting pet when it was young, but as it grew up it became more and more mischievous until it became a
nuisance. Everytime one of the children would get
out in the yard, the antelope would slip up behind
and butt the child over, and then he would scamper
off in great glee. We finally had to kill him.

In January, 1890, we had a big snow storm which
continued for thirty-six hours, covering the ground
six inches deep. During the storm the cattle in the
west pasture drifted into a pocket in the fence about
three miles south of Singer's Store. As soon as the
storm subsided I took several hands to drive the cattle back to the canyon where they would have more
shelter. We found about 5,000 cattle and 3,000 antelope lodged in the pocket. The driving turned out to
be a bigger job than we anticipated, for all the antelope were snow-blind, and their eyes were frozen
over with snow. It took two days to drive the cattle
three miles because of the antelope. They were in
their way. We would kick them and whip them with
our quirts, but to no avail. We had to weave in and
out among them and separate the cattle from them
the best we could.

In the spring of 1890 a real estate man by the
name of W. E. Rayner came to Lubbock County and
began to talk about laying off a townsite and estab-
lishing a county seat. None of us had thought about
such a thing up to that time. There was not a town

in the county, and only one store. George W. Singer
was still operating his store in Yellow House Canyon. His first store was burned in 1886. A demented
Mexican had set it afire one day while Singer was
away. Singer returned just as the Mexican was flee-
ing from the building. He killed the Mexican, but
was unable to save the store. Singer then hauled lumber from Colorado City and built another store about
half a mile down the Canyon from his old site.

Rayner was a professional town promoter. He had
located a townsite which he hoped to make the county seat of Stonewall County, named the town after
himself, built a courthouse which he intended to sell
to the county, and put on a lot sale. Nobody came to
buy, and a rival town, Aspermont, got the county
seat. Mr. Rayner, left with a courthouse on his hands,
was not put out. He started looking for new county
seats to locate, and settled on Lubbock County. He
figured that a town located near the middle of the
county would have no trouble getting the county seat,
especially if it were the only town in the county.

He selected the section of land which now lies
directly north of the Tech Campus, surveyed a townsite, and named it Monterey. He wanted the good
will of some of the local citizens, and offered Frank
(F. E.) Wheelock and myself ten lots each if we
would support him in his effort to get the county
seat at Monterey. Wheelock and I had been watching
his activity, and had decided that the matter of starting a town was not so involved. We told him our
support would cost a great deal more than ten lots

apiece. He got mulish and said that was all he would give. Wheelock and I decided to start a town of our own.

We purchased the section of land which lies just east of the Plainview highway and north of the Canyon. We saw it was going to take more money than we had to launch the town, so I went to Fort Worth and interested John T. Lofton and James Harrison in the project. They furnished the money and we four became equal partners. We laid out the townsite and named it Lubbock, after Captain Thomas S. Lubbock of Texas Revolutionary fame. We built the Nicolette Hotel and a store building, dug a well, and erected a windmill. In the meanwhile we were lining up the voters in the county to vote for Lubbock for the county seat.

The outlook was getting pretty gloomy for Rayner. He began to have visions of another town without inhabitants or a county seat. In December, 1890, he came to us with a proposition for a compromise. We dickered around for awhile and finally came to an understanding. We agreed to purchase a section of land on the south side of the Canyon equidistant from our town and Rayner's town. The new town was to be laid out on the same plan as Monterey, but was to have the name of Lubbock. Rayner took the north half of the townsite, and Lofton, Harrison, Wheelock and I took the south half.

J. D. Caldwell was the first merchant to open a store in the new Lubbock, and a short time later G. W. Singer moved up from the Canyon. During Janu-

ary and February, 1891, we were busy moving the
town. We had to tear the hotel down to get it across
the canyon. Lofton and Rayner put on a publicity
campaign, and in the spring held a lot sale. By June
there were a dozen families living in the town, and
on July 21 Bob Rodgers started the *Lubbock Leader*.
Bob was a natural-born booster, and called on the
rest of us to support his paper while he whooped it
up for the town. Wheelock, on behalf of the townsite company, took a hundred and fifty subscriptions,
I took fifty, and every puncher on the I O A Ranch
took three each. We had made Wheelock manager
of our half of the townsite, because Lofton, Harrison, and I had no time to devote to it. Wheelock soon
began to receive letters from all parts of the United
States, wanting to know about the country.

A man by the name of J. P. Lewis had started a
saloon in Monterey (everybody called it Ray Town),
and when we compromised on the present site of
Lubbock, Lewis moved his saloon. I soon saw that a
saloon within eight miles of the ranch headquarters
was not going to add anything to the morale of the
hands. I had drunk my part of the whiskey, but I
had always made a point of keeping whiskey and
business separated. I had never allowed the punchers
to keep liquor on the ranch. After Lewis opened his
saloon in Lubbock, some of the boys would slip off
at every opportunity and get tanked up. When I
sent them to the West Pasture, they would ride several miles out of their way to get a drink of whiskey.
For fifteen to twenty-five cowboys to kill time in

that way meant a big outlay for the company, so I decided to get rid of the saloon. I circulated a local option petition, and got enough signers to carry it, as most of the newcomers were prohibitionists. In that way Lubbock went dry within three months after the town started. I gave Lewis a job on the ranch and he made a good hand.

With a town in the county, I began buying a part of the supplies for the I O A Ranch from local merchants. Notwithstanding goods had to be hauled from Colorado City, a distance of one hundred and thirty miles, or from Amarillo, a little more than a hundred and thirty miles, prices in Lubbock were not as high as one might think. Bacon sold at ten cents a pound; potatoes, at two and a half cents; syrup, at sixty cents a gallon; flour, at $2.60 a hundred; onions, at three cents a pound; stove pipe, at twenty cents a joint; nails, at six cents a pound; pecans, at ten cents a pound; apples, at fifteen cents a dozen, and oranges at twenty cents a dozen.

When a postoffice was established at Lubbock in 1891, the mail came from Colorado City three times a week. A postoffice had been established at Singer's Store in 1884, but then the mail was brought out only once a week.

No sooner had we got a town in Lubbock County than we started talking about a railroad. Our talk did not amount to much until April, 1893, when a rumor spread through the county to the effect that the Texas Central was planning to build on northwest from Albany. Then we got busy. We had several mass meetings at the livery stable in Lubbock. The big question was how we could induce the rail-road company to build to Lubbock. It was evident that Plainview, Estacado, and Espuela on the Spur Ranch in Dickens County would be contenders for the road. Should we coöperate with these towns or go at it alone? We eliminated Plainview from the coöpera-tive idea at once on the grounds that the Central would not likely build to both places. If we got the road, Plainview wouldn't; if Plainview got it, we wouldn't. So it was clear that we would have to fight Plainview. But Estacado and Espuela were different. It was possible that the Central could be induced to come by both places and on to Lubbock. So we de-cided to offer to coöperate with them. I was selected to find out about Espuela. I wrote Fred Horsbrugh, manager of the Spur Ranch and chief promoter of Espuela. Horsbrugh replied that he understood that the Central did not intend to build to any existing towns, but purposely intended to miss them so that the railroad company could establish its own towns and clean up a lot of money on the sales. In that case the existing towns would be killed, and the people would move to the new railroad towns. That sounded mighty discouraging, but caused Lubbock to become even more determined to get a railroad, as a matter of self-preservation.

The next mass meeting voted to send Judge W. D. Crump and myself to Waco to interview the officials of the Texas Central. The meeting made up $35 to pay our expenses. We drove to Albany in a buggy,

put our horses in a livery stable, and went to Waco
on the train. We put up at the Royal Hotel and
called on Colonel Hamilton, the president of the
Central. We couldn't see him that day, but were told
to be back next day. When we got an audience, he
was very nice to us and kept us for two or three
hours, asking a thousand and one questions about the
country. Then he told us we were too early, as the
Central did not intend to do any more building for at
least two years. When we got home, and made our
report, the railroad fever died down for awhile, but
not for long.

The I O A Ranch, like its neighbors, had trouble
in keeping an adequate number of saddle horses.
About two hundred and fifty were required for regular work. A horse was not fit for cow work until he
was four years old. Then after eight or ten years of
service, he would have to be replaced. In 1887 the
company had purchased one hundred mares with the
intention of raising its own horses. These stock mares
were raised in East Texas and were gentle enough
when they were brought out; but mustangs soon got
with them, and they became wild. Everytime we
wanted to get them corralled, we had to run them
down. The outcome was so unsatisfactory that in
1889 the directors of the company sent instructions
for us to trade the mares for saddle horses, but no
one cared to trade. A number of other ranches attempted to raise their own saddle horses during the
80's, but it did not take them long to discover
that it was cheaper to buy their saddle horses out-

right from regular horse ranches farther east. The
Plains region was not adapted to horse raising, especially as long as there were mustangs in the country.

The mustangs in the I O A pasture not only gave
trouble in regard to the stock mares, but, from time
to time, lured away our saddle horses. In the spring
of 1889 we were holding a round-up on the spot
where Lubbock now stands. One morning the wrangler reported a big sorrel missing from the *remuda*. I
had an idea that he had gotten off with the mustangs.
As soon as I got the boys at work on the round-up, I
started to look for the sorrel. In about five miles I
came in sight of a bunch of mustangs and some distance to one side was the sorrel. When a tame horse
attempts to join a bunch of wild horses, the mustangs
will not let him come close for a day or two. I suppose they try to prove him before they initiate him,
as it were. As soon as the mustangs sighted me, they
started to run, and the sorrel fell in about a hundred
yards behind. I put my horse at full speed in an
effort to head him off. If he got by me, it meant I
might have to run him for days. When I saw I
couldn't head him off, I drew my .45 and shot at
him. The bullet hit him on the jaw and, for some
reason, did little damage. The instant he was hit the
horse whirled around and ran like blazes back to
the round-up ground and joined the *remuda*. The
scar from the spent bullet stayed on his jaw as long
as he lived.

There were two bunches of mustangs in our pas-

ture. One bunch ranged about where Tech Campus
is now, and the other, eight or ten miles farther
south. There were about twenty wild horses in each
group. In the summer of 1889 I decided to rid the
range of these troublesome mustangs. I divided the
boys into two groups, had each man mount a good
horse, and sent a group after each bunch of horses.
The boys were to kill every mustang.

There were two men along who rode wild and
reckless. They were always hard on the horses they
rode, and on a chase like this the chances were they
would well-nigh kill their mounts. We had two old
outlaw horses which I did not care if they did ride
to death. I gave one outlaw to each man and told
them to ride as hard as they wanted to. One man
went with one group of punchers, and the other went
with the other group. About eleven o'clock that day,
about the same minute as well as we could ascertain,
both horses dropped dead while being ridden at full
speed; at the time they were about fifteen miles apart.
Neither rider was hurt in the fall. Before night the
boys had slaughtered every mustang in the pasture.

Getting rid of old, broken-down saddle horses was
another problem for the ranch. Sometimes we were
able to sell them to horse buyers who shipped them
to East Texas or Louisiana and sold them to cotton
farmers. In 1893 I decided to speculate a little in
broken-down saddle horses. I purchased thirty head
from the company at $20 each. I drove the herd to
Colorado City and shipped them to my brother-in-
law in Colbert, Indian Territory. He tried to sell

them and couldn't. Finally he traded them for thirty jersey cows, and shipped them to Amarillo. I held the cows there for three weeks, but people in the Panhandle were not interested in jersey cattle in 1893. At last, I traded them for thirty lots on Polk Street. I kept the lots for a couple of years and sold them for $7.50 apiece. I understand that some of these lots have sold in recent years for several thousand dollars each. In all, I lost several hundred dollars, besides a lot of time, but I got some good experience in horse-trading.

During 1889 and 1890, a great many farmers were preëmpting school lands on the Plains, fencing their places, building dugouts or small boxed houses, and plowing fields. They were lucky if they got a good crop before a series of drouthy years began in 1891. That year was so dry that only a small crop was made. The next year was worse, practically nothing being raised. The third year of the drouth, 1893, was a total failure. More than half the farmers starved out and had to leave the country. The drouth hung on until mid-summer, 1894. Cattlemen were suffering, but their woes were small compared with the farmers who had no reserve and no credit.

In the summer of 1894 I drove to Amarillo in a two-horse buggy on business. About the time I arrived it started raining. For twenty-four hours it poured down in sheets. As soon as the clouds cleared away I prepared to start home. I had run across the editor of the Lubbock newspaper in Amarillo, and he wanted to ride back to Lubbock with me. The whole country was flooded. The lakes were all full and running over. They were all draining towards the southeast. Occasionally, we would come to expanses of water a mile, two miles, or five miles across, and we would have to drive far out of our way to get around these lakes. Sometimes we would drive for miles through water a foot or two deep.

In April of the next year, 1895, I had another experience with the elements during a trip to Amarillo. Frank Wheelock and I were going in a buggy to Amarillo to take the train to Fort Worth. We were only a few miles from Lubbock when a sandstorm blew up, straight out of the north. The wind got harder and harder, and our horses could hardly travel at all. We let the buggy top back flat to keep it from being torn off. Then we had to hold our hats on. When we got to McWhorter's place in Hale County we had to stop. McWhorter lived in a two-story adobe house. The walls would sway in and out for two or three inches. I was afraid they would fall in, but Mr. McWhorter said there was no danger of that. During the night his windmill blew over. The next morning the wind had quieted a little, and we started on. When we got to Amarillo we found it had snowed there. The drifts were ten feet deep in places, but all the streets north and south were swept as clean as a floor.

We were gone to Fort Worth three days and then returned to Amarillo, where we got our horses and buggy and started home. On the return trip we saw windmills down all over the country. There were three down on the I O A Ranch. The new, framed courthouse at Lubbock was so careened and twisted that the doors would not shut; and the roof had to be taken off before the building could be squared again. The cook at the Nicolette Hotel told me afterwards that while the sandstorm was at its worst, he could hardly touch the cookstove because of so much electricity in the air. I have seen lots of sandstorms during my fifty-two years in West Texas, but I never saw another that could equal that one.

The ranching venture of the Western Land and Live Stock Company was never profitable. The company stocked when cattle prices were high. Scarcely had the range been stocked when prices took a long tumble. A two-year drouth was setting in. Before the pastures were completely fenced, blizzards sent thousands of I O A cattle drifting to the Colorado or the Pecos country. Many of these were not recovered for three or four years, and some were never brought back. The company was at a great expense fencing and watering the range. Prices continued to fluctuate slightly at an average level of about half what they were when the ranch was stocked. In 1891 another drouth began. By 1893 the directors of the company were hopelessly discouraged. In the spring of that year the board seriously considered disposing of the cattle and colonizing the lands. It is highly probable that had S. W. Wheelock not died a few weeks later the company would have attempted a colonization program similar to those later carried out by other large ranches in this part of the state. After Mr.

Wheelock's death the company decided to dispose of the cattle and sell the land in a body.

The directors gave us three years to get rid of the cattle. Our policy was to sell off all the yearlings each year, and as many of the other classes of cattle as we could. The T Anchor people purchased most of our young cattle. They had a range in the Dakotas to which they shipped two-year-olds, and grazed them until they were fours; then they sold to the northern markets.

I bought the last remnant of cattle from the I O A Company for less than $8 a head, and immediately sold the cattle, 7,420 head, to J. M. Daugherty of Abilene, Texas. Mr. Daugherty leased the I O A pasture for a year and employed me as his manager. He intended to hold the cattle only until he could dispose of them to some advantage. In the meanwhile he drove another herd of 5,600 head he had purchased from J. C. Beal into the I O A pasture. In October, Daugherty directed me to drive the Beal cattle to Colorado City. I divided the cattle into two-trail herds. I bossed one herd and took the lead. Deve Harrington was in charge of the second herd and followed close on my trail.

The next morning after we started, a fog came over, so dense and heavy we could not see fifty feet in any direction. Our course lay south until we came to the road from the T Bar Ranch to Colorado City; then we were to follow the road which veered southeast. The fog was so dense all day I was afraid we would cross it. When time came to camp I had to send a man up to the front to tell the point men (the two men at the head of the column) to throw the herd off the trail. The next morning the fog had lifted so that we could see two or three hundred yards. I was afraid we had lost some cattle during the night or the day before, so we counted them as we strung them out on the trail next morning; not one was missing.

I told the point men to keep a sharp lookout for the road; and when the herd was on the way, I turned back to see how the second herd was faring. I had not gone over two miles until I met the point men. Harrington and I decided he had better take a count of his herd. Our tallies showed his cattle to be intact.

The weather was fair that day and the next, but the fourth day out it began to rain. For three days and nights it fell without ceasing. The boys' slickers and tarps began to leak, and all the bedding got wet. Everybody was cold, wet, and miserable. The wood was soaked, and the cook had a hard time getting anything cooked. It was during times like this that cowhands swore they would never punch cattle again. But when we finally got to Colorado, and the boys got dry and warm, with a big meal and several drinks of whiskey inside them, they forgot about their recent resolutions. This was the last drive I ever made to Colorado City.

Daugherty soon shipped 864 head of the I O A (they were branded Cross C), and he sold the remaining 6,556 head to some parties in Kansas City

for $12.50 a head. The transaction was based on
"book count," and not on the number of cattle actually delivered by Daugherty. Many deals had been
made on "book count and range delivery" during the
peak of '83 and '84. But with memories of what had
happened since '85, cattlemen had long since ceased
to do business on a basis of "book counts". Mr.
Daugherty must have done some clever maneuver-
ing to get the people he sold to in Kansas City to
accept his figures. We delivered the cattle to the
Magnolia Pasture in Borden County in March, 1896.
This ended my connection with the I O A Ranch.
The company afterwards sold the lands to the Koker-
nots of San Antonio.

CHAPTER XV

COWBOYS

I HAVE known a lot of cowboys in my day. During the twelve years I was a ranch manager I hired and fired several hundred of them. There were all kinds of characters; young kids from the settlement downstate, grizzled old sinners who had gone up the trail during the roaring 70's and had played faro, drunk hard liquor, danced with notorious dance-hall women, and shot out the lights in Fort Dodge and Ogallala, and all the other types that fall in between. I have found there is a great deal of difference in punchers and in outfits. One crowd will have a herd at a round-up as wild as coyotes for three days, and another crowd will have the same herd as tame as milch calves within the next three days. The temperament of the punchers in an outfit is determined to some extent by the temperament of the boss. A hurrah boss will have a hurrah crowd, and an easy-going boss will have an easy-going crew. I once knew of a boss by the name of Buck Scott who could take the wildest beef herd and have them gentle and easy to handle within a very few days.

209

The number of men employed by a ranch varied from month to month during the various seasons of the year. The number of hands needed from December to April was usually about half the number employed from April to December. The extra men put on in April were usually transients who spent the winters with their families back east. About sixty-five per cent of these transients worked for us only one season; about twenty per cent returned and worked a second season; and about five per cent would work longer than three seasons.

As a rule, more cowboys appeared in the spring than we could use. We always had a number of green, over-grown country boys to arrive. Some had bullied their folks into letting them come. All of them had been lured away by the same longings that had caused me to run away in 1873 to join the Wegefarth Expedition.

I recall one boy by the name of Jim Oden. He was nothing but a kid when he came to the I O A Ranch; and I liked his manner so well I employed him. Small, wiry, good natured, he started learning cow work. I never saw a person master the art so quickly. In three months he was a top hand, and in two years he was range boss for the V V N outfit.

Somehow, I always had a kindly feeling for these young striplings bent on becoming cowboys. Most of them could be depended upon to act the fool, but the chances were that they would eventually get over that. In fact, it was probable that most of them would have the fool knocked out of them shortly. If I could not give them work, I gave them the best advice I could and sent them on.

I remember a story which a puncher told me once as to how he got the fool knocked out of him. His name was "Stony", short for Stonewall. He had worked in Wyoming and Colorado before coming to Texas. He had been with us for a month or two, but I knew very little about him until he and I took an all-day ride together once. We got to talking about the characteristics of young cowboys and he told me this story: "We had been breaking broncs for a month, and I was stove-up, and maybe a bit foolish about the head yet. You must not gather from that that I had developed enough nerve to get up on a bronc and lift the blinds myself, for I hadn't. I had been a sort of portable snubbing post, and when nothing of that kind was needed, I sat on the top rail of the fence and did the talking. I made no claims as a bronc buster, and was only a passable snubbing post; but when it came to telling how it ought to be done, I was immense.

"There was a time, however, when I yearned to be a rider. It was way back in the 70's when I was working for a big horse outfit in Colorado. Every month we took a bunch of horses into Denver to be auctioned off. Some were broke and some were not. It was the rule of the corral where the sales were held that every animal offered for sale had to be ridden. When one of our *vaqueros* successfuly handled one of the 'some were nots', a round of applause came from the crowd which always attended the sales.

"It was at these times that I longed to be a rider. How I longed for the cheers, smiles, and beer which admiring city people showered on the knights of the leather. Of course, I enjoyed a little reflected glory from the fact that I was the friend and intimate of the heroes, but that did not satisfy me. I wanted to be one of the great, to be petted and pampered by grown people, and pointed to with awe by the kids. But hard experience on numerous occasions at the ranch had taught me that if I stayed on top of a bouncing bronc, it would be only by scratching leather.

"The next best thing to being a good rider, I thought, was to convey the impression that I was good, and I set to work on that theory. On one trip we had an old pinto that was the greatest bluffer I ever saw. As soon as the lariat touched his neck the circus began. When a saddle was put on him and he was given some rope before the rider mounted, he would rear and tear and put on an exhibition of fancy pitching that was hard to beat. Then when the buster topped him, he would give a buck or two, and after that a child could handle him. My idea was: When he was roped at the sale and a rider called for, I would volunteer. He would put on his show and give the impression of being the toughest horse in the corrals. I would make the most of all the preliminaries, and the crowd would think I must be a great buster to try such an ornery cuss. Then I would mount and he would give a jump or two, and the spectators would get the idea that I had conquered him.

"There was an immense crowd present when the occasion arrived; some were wanting to buy horses, and some were looking for fun and excitement— and they got what they came after. When Old Pinto's turn came, a rope was thrown on his neck, and I started through the mud with my saddle and blinds. By a few judicious cuffs and kicks I got him to throw a couple of fits. He snorted, pawed, reared, and pitched. Cheers and yells arose from the crowd. I heard them saying, 'I'll bet he's a rider', 'ain't he nervy', 'so cool about it.' My chest went out about six inches, and I could hardly keep my mind on what I was doing for listening to the comments. That was my great moment. The impression I had longed for was about to be made. Of course, Old Pinto wasn't going to do anything, but the crowd would always believe that I could have ridden him if he had.

"I carefully adjusted the blinds, pulled my cinches up, went into the saddle, and lifted the petticoats from his eyes. Whether it was the strange proceedings, or the surroundings, or the crowd, I am unable to say, but that old horse evidently thought it an extraordinary occasion and he was expected to do his part—and he did it.

"The first jump I got a birds-eye view of Denver; on the second, a panorama of the Platte Valley unrolled before me. It was on the return trip to earth from the second jump that I made my impression— about twenty feet ahead of Old Pinto. As I dug the adobe out of my ears, I heard the cheers that I had longed for. Somehow, they lacked the right sound. They were hearty enough; but, heaven knows, there was something wanting about them. I have since read that pride goes before a fall. I can't vouch for that; but I know it departs after a fall. To add insult to injury, a fellow in the garb of a miner waded out and looked at the 'impression' and said, 'If you will square the corners and timber her up you could hold the corral under the assessment law.' Another party, a Mormon from up about Greeley, said, 'If you'd try'er again and manage to hit in the same place, you'd get water, shore.'

"After that, I didn't need any fame or trimmings; the solitude of the ranch was good enough for me."

"Stoney" and I had not gone far after he finished this story until we crossed the sandy bed of Double Mountain River. At one side near the bank we saw a frazzled notebook like that some punchers carried in their pockets. I rode over, picked the notebook up, and found it contained a part of a cowboy's diary. The place had evidently been the scene of a desperate conflict. The sand was pawed up, and scattered around were some leather fringe from a pair of leggings, a collar torn from a shirt by main force, and a small section of a man's ear which might be described as an "underbit". Everything seemed to indicate that a "scrapping" match had been conducted on a go-as-you-please basis; we were puzzled at first to account for the state of affairs, but after reading the last few pages of the diary, we knew fairly well

who the combatants were. The entries which had a
bearing on the subject were as follows:

March 15—Started to pullin' bogs today, me and
a nigger. Camped two miles above the widder woman's.

March 16—Eat dinner at the widder's today. She
has got 300 head cattle and a dawter. All shorthorns.
Widder's name is Jackson; dawter's name is Maud.

March 17—Found one uv old man Brown's cows
bogged today. She is bogged yet. I am sorry for the
old sister, but Brown fired me last year.

March 18—Saw old Rattlesnake today. He is
fattern as a fule. Ain't been rid in a year. Guess I
will mash him pretty soon.

March 19—Eat dinner at the widder's agin today.
Bill hardin was there. I axed him up to camp, but he
said he doin' pretty well.

March 20—Found one of the widders cows bogged today. Worked all day gettin' her out. Goin' to
take her home tomorrow.

March 21—Took the cow home. Bill hardin is
there yet. Looks like that fule would get a job an
not be a eatin' the bread of widders and orphins.

March 22—Brung old Rattlesnake in tonight.
Goin' to drag it out uv him tomorrer.

March 23—(No entry.)

March 24—Got throwed yesterday. Twiest.

March 25—there is goin' to be war. harding told
the widder I druv that cow in the bog and then got'er
out and druv her home to play solid. I am goin' to
pessle hardin' til he hollers.

March 26—Past the widders today and didn't get axed in. That is hardin's work.

March 27—Boss here today. Said he had hired hardin' to run his waggin this summer. I am goin' to quit on the furst. Got to lick hardin' fore I do.

March 28—The thing comes off tomorrow.

There were no further entries. However, we saw Harding at the ranch next day, and his ear showed no evidence of having been "underbitten." Aside from a long scratch on the neck, probably caused by a spur rowel, he showed no signs of having been in the recent tussle; so we had a pretty good idea as to how the "thing" had terminated.

All tenderfoot punchers had a notion that the first prerequisite for becoming a regular hand was ability to stay on top of a bucking horse; and they worked manfully to achieve that. Only a few ever became expert riders, the great majority becoming only tolerable ones. The next ambition was to become a top rope man. That distinction was one to be envied. At a round-up where thirty or forty men were working, the top rope men stood out sharply above the rest. The young cowhand literally spent days and weeks, and months practicing with the rope. As in the case of riders, expert ropers were few. In thinking back over the great ropers I have known, I believe the list is headed by Joe Stokes, who worked during the early 80's for the Long S outfit and later for the Spurs. Then there was Handy Cole, of the Spur Ranch, who did a lot of "reping" in the Square and Compass country. Van Sanders, of the "22" Ranch, was mighty good, and Tom Harrison of the Spurs could wield a lariat, as well as cards in a poker game, to a fare-you-well. It seemed that the Spur outfit had a corner on the ropers. I was not any slouch myself in my younger days, but after I got my shoulder stove up, I never tried to compete any more.

There was a transient who came through the country and worked for the Square and Compass awhile who was also hard to beat. We called him Snaky; I never knew why unless it was because he handled his tall, slim, wiry body when riding, roping, or branding, gracefully like a snake a-crawling. He was an honest-to-goodness top hand; the trouble was he would never stay in one place long enough to do any good. He was restless-like, and as soon as he got a little money ahead, he always drifted on.

I marveled at Snaky's ability to rope. One day while we were loafing at a line camp, I persuaded him to give a little exhibition and show me some of the fine points of his skill. We rode out to where some cattle were grazing. Before he started roping, he showed me how he swung a rope and made a few fancy shots, throwing the lasso from or to any point, over either shoulder, behind or in front. Then he made a pass at a big bull, who looked surprised and started off like a steam engine, but Snaky's pony planted his feet firmly in the ground and checked Mr. Bull in his mad career before he got well started. The lunge didn't throw the bull, and he went round and round, as the horse pivoted. It is

mighty hard to throw a large animal by the horns;
so Snaky neatly worked the loop loose and flipped
the lariat from the bull's horns. Then Snaky began
to exhibit what he could do. He could put a loop
just in front of a steer's foot, while horse and steer
were going full blast, just in time for the steer to step
in it. As quick as lightning he would tighten the rope
with a sudden jerk, his pony would swing, and the
steer would roll over in the dust. Snaky could put
the loop in front of either forefoot or hindfoot and
never miss. He would start the noose with a few
quick whirls, and then it would shoot to the place
at which he aimed like a bullet from a revolver.

A few days later we had a little roping match at
a round-up. The contestants were to cut a steer from
the herd, rope, throw, and tie the animal. Van Sanders made the best record; his time was two minutes
and ten seconds. Snaky came second; his time was two
minutes and forty seconds. However, his first lariat
broke, and he had to untie another from his saddle
and make a second catch.

A good many negroes worked on the ranches in
this part of the state. They were employed as cooks,
horse wranglers, and bronc busters. Jordan Rollins
worked for us on the I O A Ranch for five years.
While we were at headquarters he broke horses, and
when on range or trail work he wrangled the *remuda*.
Tall, rawboned, long-legged, and loose-jointed, Jordan could ride broncs with less exertion and more
ease than any buster I ever saw. Jordan had a way
with broncs. He would spend hours working with a

horse before he saddled him, putting a blanket on and taking it off a hundred times.

Jordan was honest, careful, dependable. He did his work well and was always doing favors for the punchers. On range and trail work I always took my turn at standing guard along with the other boys. Jordan always insisted on standing his turn and mine too. If anyone felt indisposed, it was Jordan who volunteered to relieve him. I paid him as much as I paid the white men. In addition, he washed for some of the boys and made a little extra, and he saved every dollar. When he went home one winter, he gave me $500 to keep for him until he got back. I understand that he later acquired considerable property in his home community.

The average puncher used a great deal of profanity. He did not do it because he had anything especially malicious against the Deity, but mostly because he wanted to be like the other punchers, and because it helped him to express himself more forcibly. I used to wonder if these fellows who took the Almighty's name in vain so often were really as irreligious as a stranger might think. I am convinced that they were not. In fact, down deep under his hide the average cowhand was religious. No one could claim he was ritualistic. He would have hooted at being called a churchman, although most of them after their punching days were over "got religion" at some camp meeting and joined the Baptist or Methodist church.

The average puncher had a respect for the supernatural forces he could not understand. Occasionally one came along with Christian professions, but he had his own notions about the application of his creed. There was Pete McSpadden, a six-footer, raw-boned, skinny and a top hand. He was a born orator, and would entertain the boys with political speeches, sermons, and, if needs be, he would pray. He was religiously inclined, and I heard he became a preacher in his later life. One night while on a round-up, we got to talking about religion, and Pete expressed his notions about it.

"Lots of folks that really want to do right, think servin' the Lord means shoutin' themselves hoarse praisin' His name. Now, I tell you how I look at that. Suppose I'm working for Jim here. If I'd sit around the house telling what a good feller Jim is, and singing songs to him, and get out in the night and serenade him when he'd rather sleep, I'd be doing jist like lots of Christians do, but I wouldn't suit Jim, and I'd get fired mighty quick. But when I button on my chaps and hustle around the hills and see that Jim's herd is all right, and ain't sufferin' for water and feed, and ain't being run off the range and being branded by cow thieves, then I am serving Jim as he wants to be served. If I was riding for the Lord, I believe He would like for me to ride out in the ravines where the common folks live and keep His herd from being branded by the Devil and run off to where the feed was short and the drinking holes were dried up, and where there would be no friendly cedar breaks or creek bluffs for shelter when the blizzards come.

"I don't see how I would be helpin' the Lord if I just laid around the ranch house eatin' up all the grub I could get and getting down on my prayer bones and taffying the Lord up and askin' for more.

"The Bible says somethin' somewhere—I've the place marked with an ace of spades—about how people serve the Lord by feedin' and waterin', and lookin' after the herd. I think it would do lots of people good to read it over. When a critter has had his moral nature starved ever since he was a calf, and was let run a human maverick until the devil took pity on him and put his brand on him so deep that even when his hair is longest in the spring no one would have any trouble telling whose herd he belonged to—it shows mighty plain that the cowpunchers of the Lord have been a-huntin' salary harder than they've been a-huntin' souls."

That's the way Pete felt about it, and sometimes he caused some of the boys to do a little thinking.

Cowpunchers had their own way of talking. They were rather sparing with words, and had a way of saying things concise and to the point. The only rule of speech they seemed to observe was to avoid "beatin' around the bush". They devised a vocabulary of their own. A cutting horse was often a "chopping horse" or a "carving horse". Riding a bronc was called "forking a horse". Looking at a horse's teeth to tell his age was "toothing". The owner of a ranch was often referred to as "the presidente"; the manager was the "boss"; the man in charge of a round-up or trail outfit was "wagon boss" or "straw boss";

a man in charge of a smaller detail of punchers was "top screw"; and common punchers were "waddies", or "screws". A man from the East who had come to learn cow work was a "short-horn", a "chuck-eater", or "arbuckle". A "stray man" was a puncher from another ranch attached to a rounding-up outfit for the purpose of gathering his employer's stray cattle. A "line-rider" was a hand who, before ranches were fenced, rode imaginary lines to keep the cattle within certain boundaries. A "fence-rider" was a cowboy employed to ride a fence and keep it in repair; a "bog-rider" was a man who rode up and down the creeks and pulled cattle out that had mired.

"Going a-gallin' " signified that a puncher was courting a girl. "Cutting a rusty" indicated that one was doing his best. "Faggin' ", or "goin' fast like the heel flies are after you", meant someone or something moving fast. A "goosey" is a man who is nervous. "Telling a windy" was telling a story. A "wind-jammer" was a person who "told windies". "I ain't got any medicine" indicated that the person did not have any information on a subject. "Anti-goglin" was going in a zig-zag way. "Sweating a game" was looking on at a game of cards, but taking no part in it. When a cowboy stayed out all night, he had "stayed out with the dry cattle". A man expert with a rope was said to "swing a cat gut" well. Riding on a cattle train instead of on a regular passenger train was "saving money for the bartender". Roping a cow was "putting your string on her". When a calf was thrown on its back with its feet up in the air it "was

sunning his moccasins". "A running iron" was a long
branding iron with a curve on one end, or sometimes
it was a large ring which a puncher carried tied to his
saddle; when hot, he handled it with a pair of wire
pliers or a couple of sticks.

There was a number of ways of describing ear-
marks. A "crop" was to cut off the end of the ear.
An "underbit left" was to cut a piece out of the
bottom side of the ear. An "overbit" was the same
thing on the top side of the ear. A "swallow fork"
was to cut a triangular piece out of each end of the
ear. A "split" was to slit one or both ears horizontally without cutting out any portion of the ear. A
"jingle bob" was to slit the ear diagonally in such a
way that the under part would flop; this mark always seemed inhumane to me. "Grub and sharp" was
to "crop" one ear off close to the head and to cut off
most of the other one, leaving what was left pointed;
this was invariably a cattle thief's mark, as it enabled
him to do away with any previous marks which the
animal may have had.

In addition to the "chuck wagon" a rounding-up
outfit sometimes had a "hoodlum wagon", a light
wagon for hauling extras such as wood, water, and
so on. The cook was a "coosey", "cosinero", "dough-
roller", or "biscuit-shooter". When he called he
yelled, "Come and get it", "chuckaway", or "come
a-running"—these calls always got results. "Pooch"
or "nigger in the blanket" was the cowboy's dessert.

A "brain tablet" was a cigarette. When a horse un-
expectedly began to buck he "swallowed his head".

If he bucked his rider off, he "turned the pack".
"Curry him out" meant to rake a horse up and down
the shoulders with the spurs. "Galves" were spurs.
To "lock spurs" was to tie a string around the rowel
so that the rowel would not turn; without doing this
the spurs did not assist the rider in staying on; on
the contrary, they acted as sort of ball-bearings in
throwing him. A "saddle roll" was a roll of blankets
tied across the saddle just behind the horn; these
helped to wedge the rider in the saddle, and made it
more difficult for the horse to throw him. "Hobble
the stirrups" was to tie them together with a rope
running from one to the other under the horse's
belly; this prevented the stirrups from flopping,
while the horse was bucking. "Ridin' 'em with a slick
saddle" was to ride a bronc without a "saddle roll"
without "hobbling the stirrups" and without "grabbing the apple"; a real buster scorned the use of any
device which gave him an advantage over the horse.
A "night horse" was one the wrangler kept staked
nearby at night to ride after the "remuda" early next
morning. The "remuda" was the saddle horses used
by a cow outfit. A cayuse was a horse, usually one for
which the rider held no admiration. If the rider of a
bucking horse had to hold to the horn (or pommel)
or any other part of the saddle, he was "grabbing the
apple" or "pulling leather".

A "sougan" was a blanket or comforter in a puncher's bed. He carried two sougans in the summer and
three or four during the winter. They were rolled up
in a tarp (tarpaulin) and the bed-roll was called a

"hot-roll" or "velvet couch". "Spool your beds" meant for the punchers to roll their beds up and tie them with a rope.

The average puncher of the 80's and 90's was inclined to be shy around women. He might be a considerable talker in a cow camp, but when he got around a lady he couldn't think of anything to say. His desire for love affairs was strong, however, and if he was short on words, he was long on any kind of action which would convey his feelings. I made the following clipping from the Taylor County *News* in 1886:

"The postmaster at Fort Keogh, M. T., who declined to vacate in favor of the woman appointed to succeed him, has been ousted in a summary manner by a cowboy admirer of the new postmistress. Eight shots were fired. Four took effect in the postmaster and none in the cowboy. The postmaster is dead. Long live the postmistress. The cowboy should now marry her, and the romance would be complete."

This event was typical of cowboy psychology. I do not mean that all punchers went around looking for postmasters to kill; this is, perhaps, the only event of this kind. This puncher probably had never said a dozen words to the postmistress, but when an opportunity came whereby he could let his feelings be known in a more tangible way, he loaded up his .45 and started in.

So much has been written about a cowboy's "togs" (wearing apparel) that I will omit them here; but there is still something to be said about saddles. In the early 70's the saddles were short, shallow, and very clumsy. They were neither comfortable nor practical for ranch use, but they had to serve the purpose, as no better ones were to be had. They had large, flat horns the size of a tin plate, eight or ten inches in diameter. They were covered with home-tanned rawhide, and strung with long buckskin strings. The stirrups were at least six inches wide and made of hickory or pecan wood.

The next style came in during the early 80's, and was called the "apple horn". The horn was almost round and about the size of a small hen's egg. The seat was deeper and the stirrups not more than half as wide as the old models. From that time on saddles were improved rapidly. Saddle pockets just behind the seat were added for carrying such miscellaneous articles as tobacco, wire cutters, lunch, or pistols. This type of saddle gradually developed into the modern saddle. The swell, or rolled, front of most modern saddles, however, is a late innovation.

Although there were saddle factories in the East, practically all the good saddles used for cow work were made in the cattle country. In West Texas the most famous saddle makers during the 80's and 90's were located at Colorado City. Farther North, Denver was the saddle-making center. In 1885 I had C. C. Blandford at Colorado City make a saddle for me. With all its trimmings, it cost $135. Among several other special features it had a soft quilted seat. This saddle was nice and comfortable for a short ride, but on a long ride it would blister the rider. For hard riding, a hard, slick seat is far better.

A good, serviceable saddle without any extra trimmings could be had for $50. The old saying about a cowboy "riding a $30 horse with a $50 saddle" was literally true. A saddle that would stand the hard usage of cattle work could seldom be bought for less than $50, and the average cowhorse was worth from $25 to $40.

The puncher's lariat was attached to his saddle horn with a leather string. During the 70's and 80's it was customary for everybody to use a stout string for this purpose. About 1888 a puncher was killed on the Long S Ranch by his spur hanging in his lariat leather. After that practically everyone in West Texas got to using a weak string, so that if he got tangled in it some way the string would break.

Spurs also underwent a development. During the 70's the shanks were long, and the rowels were at least two inches in diameter. Many of them were adorned with small bells, which would jingle continuously. These spurs were clumsy and not so practical. Later the shanks became shorter and the rowels smaller.

Along with the changes in saddles and spurs came another change. The 70's and early 80's might be called the age of rawhide and the period since the 80's, the age of wire. Before the introduction of wire, if anything broke on a ranch like a wagon tongue or a single tree, it was fixed with rawhide. The hand would cut a strip of rawhide, wet it, and wrap the broken object securely. When the rawhide dried, it was as tight as a drum. After the introduction of wire, rawhide ceased to be used as a repairing material.

There is as much difference in cow horses as there
is in cowboys. One horse may look pretty much like
another to a stranger, but to a puncher who knows
his mount, every horse has its own individuality.
Real top horses are as scarce in a cow outfit as top
hands, but it is seldom that a top hand is found without a top horse.

So much has been written about cow horses and
horse nature that I will not go into that. I differ with
Will James, however, as to how horses should be
broken. His method is to work carefully and long
with the horse, getting him as gentle as possible
before riding him. That method is all right, but it
was not practical in West Texas fifty years ago. We
did not have time to work for days with a horse before topping him. When time is an element, the best
way to conquer a horse is to treat him rough for the
first three or four days; and after that, be good to
him. The first thing we did to a bronc was to saddle
and ride him. We didn't make any petting party of it
either. When he started bucking, we gave him the
"locked spurs" and whipped him with a quirt. About
three ridings cured the average horse of his bucking. He might pitch some thereafter when first saddled in the morning, but he did not buck with the
intention of dismounting the rider.

One of the most essential traits for a bronc rider
was plenty of self-assurance. If a buster ever got
afraid of a horse, the horse seemed to realize it even
more quickly, sometimes, than the rider himself. In
that case, the affair usually terminated by the horse's

conquering the rider instead of the rider's conquering the horse.

There was a way to keep a horse from bucking at all. One could take a forked stick, fasten the forks under the horse's jaw, and tie the other end between the horse's front legs to the girth. The horse could not get his head down. Regular busters never used this method, for the best way to master a horse is to let him get his pitch out.

Once in a great while, a bronc rider found an outlaw that could hardly be conquered at all. I tackled one back in 1872 in Grayson County. We called him Old Gobbler. Two different busters had already tried to break him and failed. I took him with some reluctance, because he had the reputation of being bad medicine. He was a sorrel, big, strong, with a bald face and stocking legs. He was a most expert sunfisher—he would twist his body while in the air so as to unseat the rider. When he bucked, he snorted and screamed. Every day for a week he pawed, kicked, squealed, and squalled. When he found he couldn't get me off any other way, he would try to bite my leg. I finally cured him of biting by hitting him on the nose. A horse's nose is one of the tenderest parts of his anatomy.

After I had worked with him for about two weeks and thought I had him fairly well mastered, I was riding him down a road one day. There was a tree about twenty feet from the road, and when we got almost even with it, old Gobbler suddenly whirled from the road and ran under that tree. I am sure he figured that was his only way of getting me off. The plan worked, and as I hit the ground he kicked me in the forehead. That was sixty years ago, and the imprint of his hoof is still on my head. So far as I know, he was never branded, but he certainly branded me. I finally conquered him by rough treatment, but he always had the soul of a devil and had to be watched.

I once had another outlaw that I called Ring Tail, a blood bay with a snip nose. He was a cayuse, and would buck when first saddled, every day of the year. He was the only horse I ever rode that would go through different stunts in bucking. He would start on a straight buck, change to a zig-zag, and then give a few "sun-fisher" bucks. After doing all of these stunts, he would grab the bits in his mouth and run until he was smothered down by a hackamore. After all this darn foolishness, he was about played out, but he could still wring his tail.

During twenty-five years of active range work, I had four top horses. In 1883-1884, I rode White Bunkum, an eight hundred and fifty pound bundle of nerves. He had been captured from the Llano outfit early in 1883 by Comanche Indians and ransomed back for $20. He was great for cutting, but he did not like roping. I suppose it was because he was so small that the lunging animal gave him too much of a jolt.

From 1885 to 1888 I rode Tallow Eye, a buckskin with a black mane and tail, and creamy eyes. He was good for riding, cutting and roping. All I had to do was to show him where the cut was being held and indicate which animal I wanted in the herd; then he would do the rest. I could drop the reins over the saddle horn, and Tallow Eye would take the animal out of the herd and to the cut.

During the same time I had in my mount Big Foot, a big blood bay. He was a good roping horse, especially with heavy cattle; but he was not so good on cutting.

The greatest of all cow horses in my experience was Gray Baby, a little gray. He was not only a good cutting and roping horse, but he loved the work. Fast and gentle, he was never happier than when working in a herd, keeping his mind on his business better than most men do. I could leave him anywhere and he would stand until I returned. When running full speed over ground containing numerous dog holes, he kept his eye on the ground, dodging and jumping. Only once in seven years did Gray Baby ever lose his footing. While cutting a steer on slippery ground, he whirled suddenly, and his feet went out from under him. He got up before I did and came to me trembling and excited. I patted him on the forehead and mounted. He went to work as if nothing had happened. A great little horse with human sense.

CHAPTER XVI

TURNS FOR THE WORSE

FOR several years before I left the I O A Ranch I had been preparing to start into the ranching business on a small scale for myself. In 1891 I had filed on a section of school land two miles north of the I O A headquarters under the "One Section Act" of 1887 at a cost of two dollars per acre. The next year I started improving the land, and by 1896 I had $10,000 worth of improvements on it. In that year the Four Section Act" was passed. In order to be eligible for taking up land under this law I had to forfeit my original section. I refiled on it in 1898, along with three other sections "within a five-mile radius". In the refiling, I got the home section for one dollar an acre instead of two. About the same time I purchased the three sections of the old Williams sheep ranch. This gave me 4,480 acres of my own and I leased another 3,250 acres. With this tract of 7,730 acres I started the Idlewild Ranch and began raising registered Herefords.

About the time I was starting Idlewild Ranch we suddenly lost two of our children from diphtheria.

Their deaths were largely due to the fact that the nearest doctor was at Plainview. By the time we sent a man horseback the fifty-five miles and the doctor drove back in a buggy, it was too late for him to do any good.

By 1897 enough settlers had come to Lubbock County for us to organize a school system. The whole county was one district. There were three trustees and three small, one-teacher schools; by mutual consent each trustee had complete control of his own school. The Groves school was the largest of the three, and was located seven or eight miles northwest of Lubbock. It had four patrons, but three of these had twenty-nine children: G. O. Groves had ten, Joe Lang, ten and Sam Gholson, nine. Mr. Groves was trustee of this school. The Young school was located about two miles west of Slaton, and Mr. Young was the trustee. I was the trustee for the Canyon School which was located two miles north of Idlewild Ranch. We had about ten pupils in 1898.

Ever since I had seen my first windmill on the Plains about 1883, I had wondered if the wind could not be harnessed to furnish power. In 1904 I decided to experiment with the idea. I purchased a huge windmill, mounted it on a seventy-five foot tower, and installed a device for transmitting the power to a feed-grinder. On the whole, the experiment was not a success. The wind was too spasmodic, and we had no way to regulate the speed of the mill. If the wind were steady and at the proper velocity, we could grind feed very well, but such occasions were rare.

In 1907 I sold the ranch for $25,000, moved to Lubbock, and began to try my hand at business. My first venture was in an automobile stage line. Three other men and myself organized a partnership and purchased four two-cylinder, chain-drive Buicks at a cost of $1,250 each. The company sent a boy from Kansas City to teach us how to drive. On our first trip we left Amarillo early in the morning and got to Lubbock late the next day. Later we got to where we could make the drive in a day, provided we got an early start and did not have any trouble; we usually had trouble, however. After a few weeks I bought out the other three partners. My first change in policy was to leave Hale Center off my route and include Plainview. It was not long until another outfit put in a line of Jackson cars in opposition to my line. I either had to quit business or buy the other line out. I did the latter, but it cost me dearly, because the Jackson cars were no good.

When the railroad reached Plainview from Canyon City in 1909, I ran my cars from Plainview to Lubbock. By that time I had traded off the two-cylinder cars and installed four four-cylinder cars at a cost of $2,750 each. I was having so much trouble with wagon freighters that I procured a private right-of-way all the way from Plainview to Lubbock. I was approaching a freighter one day and his horses began to rear and try to kick out of the traces before I got within a quarter of a mile. The freighter jumped out with his Winchester and motioned for me to go around. I did, and made the circle a big one. I got the right-of-way by making arrangements with the landowners whereby I was to put in stock-guard crossings at the fences, and grade the road. Only the landowners and I were to use it. I graded two roads side by side, and used one for dry weather, and one for wet weather. When the railroad reached Lubbock in 1909, I sold my cars and retired from the bus business.

Since then I have dabbled in a number of enterprises, and have always come out at the little end of the horn. Among other things I was county tax assessor for fourteen years. Somehow, a tax assessor's job is one that most broke cowmen seem to come to sooner or later. As long as I stayed in the cattle business I prospered, but when I left the only vocation I knew, every venture that I made was for the worse.

(THE END)

INDEX

237